Protect & Prosper!

PROTECT &DEFEND

Published by CelebrityPress™, Orlando, FL
A division of The Celebrity Branding Agency®

Celebrity Branding® is a registered trademark
Printed in the United States of America.

ISBN: 9780985364311
LCCN: 2012936234

This publication is designed to provide accurate and authoritative information with regard to the subject matter covered. It is sold with the understanding that the publisher is not engaged in rendering legal, accounting, or other professional advice. If legal advice or other expert assistance is required, the services of a competent professional should be sought. The opinions expressed by the authors in this book are not endorsed by CelebrityPress™ and are the sole responsibility of the author rendering the opinion.

Most CelebrityPress™ titles are available at special quantity discounts for bulk purchases for sales promotions, premiums, fundraising, and educational use. Special versions or book excerpts can also be created to fit specific needs.

For more information, please write:

CelebrityPress™
520 N. Orlando Ave, #2
Winter Park, FL 32789
or call 1.877.261.4930

Visit us online at www.CelebrityPressPublishing.com

PROTECT
&DEFEND

Contents

CHAPTER 1

Common IRS Myths

By Cary B. Bryson, Attorney at Law

I meet people everyday whose stories would make you cry. They're real, well-meaning people like you and me. They have jobs, kids, mortgages and are productive U.S. citizens. They're your friends and neighbors. They want to pay their fair share of taxes and follow the rules. Yet the circumstances of life just get in the way.

Here's a classic example. I recently visited with a man whose business burned to the ground. Then a few weeks later he had a close family member hospitalized, and his house flooded. There's more! Then he had another close family member go "missing." This all happened within a few months! As you can imagine, filing his tax returns and paying his taxes weren't a priority. They weren't even on his radar. He was simply surviving and trying to muddle through a very, very rough spot!!

After a while he began to function normally and get his life together. His business began to operate normally, and he could lift his head from his pillow in the morning with hope. Just as he began to "breathe," he had an IRS revenue officer show up on his doorstep. He tried for several weeks to work with the IRS officer—with very little success. The officer showed little or no compassion and ultimately began levying his personal and business bank accounts. That's why he ended up in my office. Eventually, I was able to help him work toward a resolution and calmer waters. He just needed help getting there.

Anyone facing an IRS visit or threatening letters has millions of unanswered questions and fears. There are as many "myths" floating around about the IRS as there are dollars. They're so widely believed, they're virtually urban legends! I'm here to bust some of the common IRS myths so you, your family, and friends can avoid needless headaches.

MYTH #1: IF I CAN'T PAY THE IRS WHAT'S DUE, IT'S BEST NOT TO EVEN FILE MY TAX RETURN.

False. You should always file your returns. Why? Simply put, because failing to file your tax return is a crime! The IRS can put you in jail for failing to file your return.

Lots of taxpayers think they can hide from the IRS by not filing their tax returns, or they think that if they don't file their returns, they don't owe the taxes. This is just flat wrong and only makes the situation worse!

First, the IRS *can't* put you in jail for failing to pay your taxes. However, you can be criminally charged and *placed in jail for failing to file your tax returns*. The current sentence can be up to one year in jail for every unfiled tax year.

Second, if you fail to file a tax return, the IRS will file one for you. This is typically called a Substitute for Return, or SFR. The IRS prepares it from a one-sided standpoint. It includes all available income and virtually no exemptions, deductions or other expenses. You're normally assessed with the maximum amount of tax possible. After preparing the SFR, the IRS will then begin collecting the inflated amount in normal ways (liens, levies, etc.).

So the next logical question becomes: *What do I do if I have unfiled returns?* Easy: *File them!*

This is the fastest way to get yourself back on track with the IRS. Begin first by consulting a trained tax preparer. Don't be intimidated; get your income and expenses and other relevant tax information together. The numbers don't have to be exact. Just do your best. Be honest and estimate based upon all available information. The IRS will usually accept best guesses.

However, don't be overly aggressive with deductions you can't prove. The last thing you need is an audit of the returns.

If you have multiple years of unfiled returns, try to prepare only one year at a time. If you try to work on multiple years at the same time, it will overwhelm you and become too stressful. Break the project into small one-year increments.

Don't mail multiple returns together. Mail separately every couple of days. This will avoid having one IRS employee receive all of your returns on the same day, which could create suspicion or even cause them to be lost.

If the IRS has prepared an SFR for you, you should protest it. Normally, the IRS will re-calculate the amount owed as stated on the return, and this will significantly reduce your taxes for that period. (We've saved clients thousands of dollars by doing this.)

Finally, don't worry if you can't pay the tax amounts stated on the returns. This is very common. *You should still file them—even if you can't pay!* Once the returns are filed and processed, the IRS will send you a letter (or bill) for each filed tax period. This is normal and is supposed to happen. Take a deep breath and wait. After you've filed all the returns and received all the bills, then you can deal with the final total amount.

MYTH #2: IF THE IRS SHOWS UP AT MY DOORSTEP, I MUST DROP EVERYTHING I'M DOING AND RESPOND TO REQUESTS IMMEDIATELY.

False. You have legal rights that must be observed by any IRS employee, including the right to common courtesy.

I can't tell you how often I hear from clients, "I was at my office and this gal from the IRS just showed up looking for me, and then started asking a million questions about my taxes and how much money I make. She threatened me with levies if I didn't pay the taxes immediately, so I agreed to a monthly payment plan, but it's just too much, and I simply can't afford it."

This IRS behavior is wrong on so many levels, it's hard for me to do it justice in this short chapter. But here are the highlights: First, you have the right to common courtesy! Who in anyone's life is entitled to just show up unannounced at another person's workplace (or home) and start making demands on them? Maybe your boss or your mom or dad, but that's a really exclusive list of folks.

Most people are so scared of the IRS, they just cave when they see the badge or the business card. They drop anything they're doing. They'll sit with that IRS person for hours answering questions, giving financial information, and making promises they don't really even know that they can keep.

The reality is these unscheduled meetings are designed to catch people off guard and unprepared so they'll voluntarily spill their guts to the IRS mostly out of fear. The bottom line is if an IRS employee drops in on you, *it's your legal right to inform him or her that you're busy and would like to reschedule the impromptu meeting to a date and time that's acceptable to both the IRS and you.*

Second, you have the right to seek legal counsel to help with your tax problems. This isn't typically something that the IRS employee will tell you. I would advise you to politely refuse to answer any questions about your tax situation and kindly say you're going to hire an attorney to help you sort this thing out, so you need to schedule another meeting.

A word of caution: If you say you're going to hire someone to help you (an attorney), you must actually do it! Putting off the meeting by invoking your right to counsel and then failing to follow through will only worsen your tax situation. It will make it harder for your attorney to help you get to the end with the IRS. Not to mention, it will erode the IRS employee's trust in you.

Finally, some food for thought. Never lie to the IRS! It's perjury, and it's a crime. Never answer a question unless you're 100 percent positive of the answer. If you don't understand or don't know the answer, just tell the IRS "I don't know or I don't recall." That's perfectly acceptable.

Finally, if you've been served with an IRS summons, you *must* appear! This isn't an impromptu meeting. A summons is a legal court order demanding your appearance on a certain date and at a certain time. Failure to appear will jeopardize your liberty (because it's a criminal act). Not only that, it will also make your tax case worse! (Of course, you should never appear unprepared or without your attorney!)

MYTH #3: AN IRS "LEVY" AND AN IRS "LIEN" ARE THE SAME THING.

False. An IRS "levy" is the actual seizure or taking of a taxpayer's property (usually money) to pay back taxes. An IRS "lien" acts like a mortgage on a taxpayer's property, but it is not an actual seizure or taking.

I had a client call me the other day freaking out saying that the IRS had filed a "lien" and was taking his house. After calming him down, I proceeded to explain the difference between the two.

Here are the basics: An IRS levy typically falls into two categories: a *bank levy* or a *wage levy (or garnishment)*. The IRS will send notice of the levy to your bank or employer, advising that you owe taxes. The levy notice will demand that your money (or a portion of it) be sent directly to the IRS to pay the taxes. There's a 21-day waiting period before the money should be sent.

This is an actual "taking" of your money, and the bank or your employer must honor the levy unless they receive an IRS release of the levy before the 21 days expire. The money will be sent directly to the IRS and will be paid toward the tax periods that the IRS deems to be in the government's best interest.

This is every taxpayer's biggest fear. It comes at the most unexpected time and is the most intrusive interruption of the taxpayer's life. Imagine getting a fraction of your paycheck due to an IRS wage levy. It's devastating.

A lien is totally different. A notice of tax lien is filed in the local courthouse. It *acts like a mortgage in favor of the IRS*. Any property owned by the taxpayer when the notice is filed and later becomes subject to the IRS lien, but it's not a "taking" like a levy.

If you own a home when the notice of lien is filed, it becomes subject to the IRS lien. The bottom line is you can't really do anything with the house (sell, refinance, etc.) unless the taxes are paid. It doesn't mean that the house now belongs to the IRS. For the IRS to "take" the house, it must go through formal seizure proceedings in the court system.

What you really need to know about levies and liens is that they're the "big sticks" used by the IRS to collect taxes. They're the No. 1 way to get a taxpayer's attention! The good news is that the taxpayer has some legal rights to prevent them—namely, by doing something and reaching an agreement with the IRS and/or filing collection appeals.

To conclude, we all know that life can sometimes get in the way of handling your taxes in a timely manner. Of course, you can't stop living your life. But you also can't hide from the IRS. Trying to "fly under the radar" may end with you losing a lot of sleep and causing endless worry. The first thing to do when you have a tax problem is to become proactive! Stop the bleeding and address the problem. Don't bury your head in the sand because of the myths you've heard about the IRS.

It's said the truth will set you free. While you may not be completely free of taxes, knowing the truth about the "mythical IRS" can help you make the best of a bad situation. Find someone who will dispel the myths and give you good tax advice in the process.

About Cary

Cary Bryson is a "no-nonsense" Louisiana attorney who has dedicated his law practice to helping people get out of IRS and other tax trouble.

Cary founded Bryson Law Firm, LLC, in 2000 with one main objective—to establish a modern law firm with old fashioned values! In other words, Cary's law firm provides great service and gets great results for its clients all while treating others with respect and dignity. He's known throughout the state as being kind, generous and friendly. (It's not uncommon for him to have two-hour meetings with new clients who drive more than three hours to meet with him!)

Simply put, Cary is a true Louisiana boy! He grew up in Baker, Louisiana. He hunts, fishes and loves to cook (and eat)! He graduated from Louisiana State University at Baton Rouge in 1988, and then from LSU Law School in 1991. With more than 20 years of legal experience, Cary has practiced in numerous legal areas throughout Louisiana. He served as a law clerk to the Supreme Court of Louisiana in New Orleans and has tried many types of cases. He's admitted to U.S. Tax Court and has extensive knowledge in IRS procedure and practice. He has handled hundreds of IRS and other tax cases.

Cary's wife, Angie, is also a Louisiana-born attorney. She works side-by-side with him at Bryson Law Firm, LLC. They've been married for 21 years and have six children who are their pride and joy.

Cary's personal dedication to "family" is reflected daily at Bryson Law Firm, LLC. His staff of lawyers, accountants and others always treat clients like family while solving their burdensome IRS and other tax issues. Bryson Law Firm, LLC clients have strong, competent protection from the IRS and other taxing agencies. Every day levies are released, garnishments are removed, and IRS cases are settled permanently for Bryson clients! It is Cary's personal goal to protect as many Louisiana neighbors as possible from intimidating and threatening IRS actions and to keep those neighbors out of tax trouble for good.

To learn more about Cary Bryson and Bryson Law Firm, LLC, or to subscribe for a free copy of his monthly newsletter, visit www.brysonlawfirm.com or call (337) 233-4210.

CHAPTER 2

2 Ways to Tackle an IRS Problem Before It Tackles You

By Nick Nemeth

Let's face it. Even the mention of the IRS makes most people cringe in much the same way as someone saying they're getting a tooth filled or getting a colonoscopy. In fact, my experience dictates that most people would opt for a colonoscopy versus having to deal with an IRS problem! But in exactly the same way as either of those necessary evils, IRS problems do arise and do need to be addressed sooner rather than later. You need to treat an IRS problem the same way would a toothache: assess the problem and address it before you lose the tooth altogether. Tackle the problem before it tackles you.

Let me share with you a couple of scenarios that might make you think twice about how you deal with the IRS. The first is an anecdote about a former client of mine who I'll call Mr. X.

My client, Mr. X, was a small-business owner who knew he was falling behind with his payroll taxes, but he didn't want to deal with the problem immediately. Like so many other business owners, he kept thinking, "I can't pay now, but I'll get caught up next time." He let it go for a couple years until one day a revenue officer left a business card on his door. He ignored that, too. Finally, Mr. X received the "bad letter" from the IRS. The IRS by law must send you adequate notification that you owe them money and that they intend to collect it. You only have 30 days to act once you receive a "Final Notice of Intent to Levy," or collection activity might quickly begin.

Mr. X was unnerved enough by his receipt of the letter that he quickly contacted my office and came in for a consultation within a week. It took Mr. X two years of delay for the IRS to catch up with him and for Mr. X to finally seek help. I advised him that he only had a few days left to file an appeal, before the IRS may begin levying bank accounts or seizing assets and receivables. Mr. X chose not to retain my firm at that meeting. We didn't hear from Mr. X again until nearly three months later when he came back to me reporting that his clients had received a notice of levy from the IRS. A notice of levy to his clients essentially meant that instead of paying Mr. X what they owed him, they must now send the money directly to the IRS!

His entire client list now had received these notices, and to make things worse, his bank accounts had been levied to pay his back taxes as well. So it's not an *intent* to levy anymore; it's an actual levy. When he returned to my office, I warned him that we might be able to quickly get some of this money back for him to run his business, but we might not.

I advised him that by delaying and ignoring my original advice from our first meeting, he had taken away some of my ability as his attorney to effectively help him. Mr. X ended up with about $150,000 being taken from him in those first several months by an overly aggressive revenue officer assigned to his case. Mr. X ended up having to shut down his company that he had spent more than 20 years building. The company also declared bankruptcy, and Mr. X now faces personal liability for his company's debts. As unfortunate as it may be, I see this happen fairly regularly to those who delay taking action.

HOW TO TACKLE AN IRS PROBLEM #1: PROMPT RESPONSE

The first way to tackle your IRS problem is don't delay! Once you have an attorney you've thoroughly vetted and in whom you trust, listen to his/her advice. The attorney isn't telling you to do certain things for no reason; he/she has you and your business's best interests at heart. Your delay could end up costing you more than money. It could cost you your business, your lifestyle and your reputation, all of which you've worked hard to build. Hiding your head in the sand won't make your IRS problems go away.

I understand that some people think that they'll never be able to "win" with the IRS. However, some people also legitimately believe that they will "get caught up" and pay off their taxes after the downturn in the economy is over. But the economy may not turn around as quickly as a person or a business owner may hope. It's best to be proactive and not wait for the other shoe to drop.

If the tomorrow you hoped for never comes and your problem doesn't get solved, then it will simply get worse. There's always a manageable solution to every one of these problems. You might be happier with one solution over another, but there's a way out and a way to stop IRS collection activity. Don't take the gamble of whether the revenue officer is going to knock on your door before you can dig yourself out from under this. By the time the revenue officer comes, it might be too late.

HOW TO TACKLE AN IRS PROBLEM #2: FILE YOUR TAX RETURNS

Lots of people, especially those who are self-employed, fall into the quagmire of not filing taxes because they know they'll owe money. Frequently, for example, a realtor might think "Oh, I didn't put aside the tax money I owe, so I'll file an extension until October and then I'll have all summer to sell another house and collect the commission so I can get the tax money together." Come October, they still don't have the money so they still don't file. This type of delay tactic inevitably seems to lead to several years of unfiled returns and a seemingly insurmountable debt.

Here's the problem: It's not a crime to owe the government money, but it *is* a crime to not file your taxes. If your thought is that you don't want to file for this year because that will tip off the IRS to the fact that you didn't file your tax return last year, you're digging yourself a crater, not a hole. Generally, this type of client comes to me and hasn't filed a tax return in 10 years because he's afraid of what might happen. At this point the client is not only facing the possibility of levies, garnishments and seizures for unpaid taxes but are also the possibility of a criminal indictment and jail time.

23

Get some advice now, not when you've become a chronic non-filer and you're facing six years of jail time. True, the IRS loves to go after the big fish like Hollywood superstars because those stories make the news. But don't falsely assume that the IRS only pursues the rich and famous. We're seeing more and more cases where the local plumber in Boise, Idaho, is going to jail for three years because he didn't file his tax returns. Moreover, when you don't file your own tax returns the IRS may take it upon themselves to prepare the missing returns for you. Do you really want the IRS preparing a return for you without giving you proper credit for your expenses, dependants, exemptions, filing status, etc.? Absolutely not.

People often ask me, *"Can I go to jail for my IRS problems?"* The answer is if you've accurately filed your tax returns, you can't go to jail, regardless of whether you owe taxes or not. That's true. But the key word here is *accurately*. You must not have given fraudulent information on your return.

People also ask, *"If you don't get advice or fail to act on that advice, what can happen?"* There's an extensive list of things the IRS can do to get their money, none of them pleasant. There can be wage garnishments and seizure of real estate, Social Security income, 401(k)s and IRAs, as well as cars, bank accounts, your home, accounts receivable, the cash value of your life insurance policy, and commissions that may be owed to you by your company.

Likewise, once a revenue officer has been assigned to your case, he has the right to talk to your employer, friends, neighbors and family. The revenue officer's job is to gather information that can be used against you in your case. Your chatty neighbor talking about your recent vacation to Europe or your new boat won't help your case. Unless you want friends and family answering questions about your job or spending habits, it's best to file your returns promptly and seek competent legal representation to keep the revenue officer off the case, or at the very least, under control.

If the threat of jail time or levying your personal or business income isn't enough to make you take action, consider the penalties that compound as a result of your inaction. You might be aware that there are financial penalties for owing the IRS money, but you may not be aware that the penalties for *not* filing may be stiffer.

47.5% PENALTY, PLUS INTEREST— ANOTHER GOOD REASON TO FILE

If you didn't file taxes for this past year, or any other year for that matter, you may be in for a very rude awakening. Interest is being compounded daily on what you owe: the quarterly federal short-term rate, plus 3 percent. As of this writing, the IRS is charging 3 percent per year.

That doesn't sound too bad... yet. But it doesn't stop there.

Non-filers are also subject to a late payment penalty each month, as well as a late filing penalty each month, and also a one-time penalty for not withholding enough taxes during the year or making required estimated quarterly payments. If this doesn't thoroughly confuse and scare you, it gets worse: Every month you don't file and pay in full, your penalties continue accruing until they cap at 47.5 percent. Ridiculous! I know loan sharks who charge less!

To put it all in perspective, if you owe $10,000 for a specific tax year and don't file or pay it for a few years, your debt could easily double to $20,000 for that year. Now multiply this amount by the number of years you haven't filed and you can now begin to imagine how a manageable problem snowballs into a monstrosity. Every day you put off taking care of your IRS problem only makes it worse.

WHAT YOU SHOULD DO IF YOU HAVEN'T FILED

By all means, file your taxes, even if you can't afford to pay the tax that's due.

By filing your taxes and not paying them, you'll at least go from Non-Filing status to Non-Paying status. This may enable you to qualify for one of the five common negotiating tactics:

1. You might be able to be declared Non-Collectible, where you pay nothing.

2. You may be able to have the debt reduced through an offer in compromise.

3. You may be able to set up a monthly installment agreement, where you pay a manageable monthly payment.

4. You might qualify for a partial-pay installment agreement (where you pay less than the total amount owed through monthly payments).

5. You may qualify to declare bankruptcy, resulting in some or all of your IRS debt being discharged through the bankruptcy proceedings

Each of the above IRS relief methods has its pros and cons, depending on the specifics of your situation.

What I hope you'll take away from reading this chapter is a sense of urgency to address whatever difficulties you're facing with your taxes and the IRS. No one likes to pay taxes. Fewer still likely enjoy the chore of assembling their information and filing their tax returns. When your birthday passes each year, you're just another year older. For each April 15th that passes where you haven't filed a return, you could be one day closer to the IRS seizing your assets and dismantling the life or business you've built.

Respond quickly when the IRS contacts you. Find a competent attorney with tax experience and heed his or her advice. If you haven't filed your taxes in years, begin with the most current year and work backward. Remember that while it's not a crime to owe the government taxes, it is a crime to not file your tax returns. Don't let yourself become Mr. X and risk losing everything and ruining your life by hiding your head in the sand and hoping your IRS problems will go away on their own. They won't.

About Nick

Nick Nemeth is a Texas attorney who's been in practice for the past 15 years. His law practice, The Law Offices of Nick Nemeth, PLLC, focuses solely on helping individuals and businesses resolve a wide range of IRS issues. Nick has been featured in *USA Today, CNBC,* *"CBS Money Watch," Yahoo Finance,* the *Miami Herald* and *Morningstar* as well as ABC, NBC, CBS and Fox affiliates around the country.

As a long-time resident of Dallas, Nick possesses a unique quality only present in those who truly love their home—a complete and personal investment in the lives of the people of his community. By creating a truly local presence in the Dallas-Fort Worth Metroplex, Nick brings his 15 years of legal experience to those who truly need it … individuals and businesses who are being threatened by the IRS.

Nick's ultimate goal in his practice, for any of his clients, is to provide efficient, cost-effective legal representation. He firmly believes that when any taxpayer is facing an "opponent" who happens to be a branch of the federal government, one who's able to seize your property and assets without going to court, that taxpayer should arm him/herself with an aggressive, experienced law firm. Nick's staff includes attorneys, CPAs, enrolled agents and tax professionals who are dedicated to keeping ahead of an ever-changing industry: solving IRS problems. Nick is known for constantly saying, "My only job is to keep the IRS as far away as possible from my clients' assets until I negotiate an acceptable solution to their problem."

Nick was driven to become an attorney by his desire to help serve others and make a positive impact on the world. He's pleased with having found a niche in which he has been able to accomplish both these goals. He loves the satisfaction of working for a diverse clientele who are unequivocally pleased with his representation. His dedication to his practice is a benefit to all in the area of law he's focused on—helping his clients solve their IRS problems.

Having traveled to places like Sweden, Austria, Denmark, Canada, Hungary and the Caribbean, Nick appreciates the ties that continue to bring him back to Dallas-Fort Worth: his law practice, his wife and five children, and the abundance of sports and community activities that keeps the family man busy.

To learn more about Nick Nemeth and his law practice, or to order a copy of his free special report, *How to End Your IRS Problems Forever*, visit www.myIRSteam.com or call (972) 484-0TAX (0829).

CHAPTER 3

Hire a Tax Attorney— and End Those Sleepless Nights

By Mary E. King, Esq.

I'm frequently at meetings, and when I'm asked what I do, and I say I'm an attorney, the person invariably asks, "What kind of attorney?" I suspect they're guessing that I'm a family and marital law attorney, because they're generally very surprised when I respond that I help people who have IRS problems. You can see the fear in their eyes as they take a step back, sort of cringe, and say something along the lines of: "You actually talk to the IRS? I could never do that."

So who am I? My name is Mary King, and yes, I'm an IRS problem-solving attorney. I've been practicing law for more than 18 years, and since 1999, my office has been located in Sarasota, Florida. The fact is my clients have all types of IRS problems that require me to talk to IRS agents on a daily basis and actually go to the local IRS office at least once a month. I have a good relationship with local IRS officials due to the fact that I've worked so many cases with them.

Although I don't have a typical client, many of them have had a traumatic experience in their life that has caused them to stop filing their federal tax returns. It may be illness, divorce, natural disaster, or the loss of a job that places filing their tax returns lower in importance than dealing with this traumatic circumstance. The problem is that once they don't file for one year, it starts to snowball, and one year becomes two and so on.

Many times, I meet with clients who have five or more years of unfiled federal tax returns. By the time a client comes to see me, something has happened in their life to make them want to get the situation resolved. For instance, they want to buy a house but can't get a mortgage because they don't have tax returns to provide to the mortgage company, they want to get married but are afraid to tell their fiancée about their tax problem, or the IRS is levying their wages or bank accounts. This is the most common type of client I represent. However, I also represent clients who've been selected for audits and don't want to deal with the IRS on their own, clients who've filed their taxes but are unable to pay them and as a result their wages or bank accounts are being levied, and businesses with payroll tax issues. You might be thinking, "How can you possibly help these clients once they've gotten themselves into such a big mess?" Fortunately, even though these IRS matters can be very painful, they also can be resolved; it just takes time, persistence and hard work.

As I indicated previously, the most common client I see has numerous unfiled tax returns. As an example, let's say that Mr. Jones retains me as his attorney. He has five years of unfiled tax returns and over the past few years has been receiving letters from the IRS advising him that he hasn't filed his returns and owes thousands of dollars in taxes. Mr. Jones is a self-employed insurance salesman, who hasn't been paying any estimated taxes. He wants to buy a house since mortgage interest rates are so low. His girlfriend is also pressuring him to get married before she purchases a house with him. However, she doesn't know about all his unfiled tax returns because he hasn't disclosed this information to her, and he receives all his mail (which includes those "friendly IRS reminder" letters) at a P.O. Box to which she doesn't have a key.

How do I help Mr. Jones? First, due to bar rules concerning client confidentiality, I communicate only with Mr. Jones and in ways that he directs to stay out of the potential hornet's nest between him and his girlfriend. He has carefully kept her in the dark regarding this matter; it isn't my place to shed light on it. Second, it's imperative that his tax returns are filed as soon as possible. The rationale is that it will take some time, and by that I mean months for the older returns to be processed through the IRS' system. Keep in mind that Mr. Jones is getting pressured not only to get married but also to buy a house, so time is of the essence. Also, the longer we wait to file his returns, the greater the possibility that his wages or his bank accounts could be seized by the IRS.

Once the tax returns are processed, we know exactly how much Mr. Jones owes. Sometimes, if the client is an employee and has had sufficient withholding taken out, they don't end up owing anything to the IRS or they may have a minimal tax debt. However, in most cases the client ends up with a significant debt for a variety of reasons. Some examples may be that they're self-employed and haven't been paying estimated taxes (like Mr. Jones), they took an early withdrawal of a 401(k) or IRA, or they didn't have enough withholding taken from their paycheck.

To resolve Mr. Jones' tax debt with the IRS, we'll have to look at the possible options available to us. Basically, a client has five options for resolving their problems with the IRS.

The first option is to pay the debt in full. Most clients, including Mr. Jones, are unable to do this.

The second option is what's called currently non-collectible (or hardship status). Taxpayers who fall into this criteria are generally either unemployed or their income is less than their monthly expenses. Currently non-collectible (CNC) is only a temporary solution, though, and the IRS will only allow a taxpayer to stay in CNC for up to 24 months before they'll review the client's financial status to see if it has improved.

A third option is a payment agreement to pay off the total debt. The amount of the monthly payment is based on the taxpayer's income and allowable expenses as determined by the IRS.

Many clients are interested in the fourth option; however, few actually qualify for the offer in compromise. The daytime TV commercials call this the settlement for "pennies on the dollar." Similar to the payment plan, the offer in compromise calculation is based on a taxpayer's income and allowable expenses, but the IRS also adds in the taxpayer's assets to the equation. Based on statistics from the IRS, only about 2 percent of all the offers in compromise submitted to the IRS are accepted.

The final option that must be considered is bankruptcy. For clients who don't have unfiled tax returns, bankruptcy may be an option. Otherwise, it may be something to consider for a later date due to timing reasons.

Getting back to Mr. Jones' situation, because his returns have just been filed, bankruptcy wouldn't be an option for him. I also indicated previously that he didn't have the funds to pay his entire debt in a lump sum. That leaves us with looking at his current financial picture to determine which of the remaining options would be best for him. After performing a thorough review of his present financial situation, which involves looking at his monthly bank statements, expenses and income, I meet with him to discuss his best settlement alternative. Because of the assets he owns and the fact that he has been very successful as an insurance salesman, when plugging in his financial information into the offer in compromise equation, he wouldn't qualify. He also wouldn't qualify for currently non-collectible because he's making more income than his expenses. As a result, I'll be contacting the IRS to set up a payment plan for him.

The benefit to my resolving the IRS problem and setting up the payment plan for Mr. Jones is that all communications go through me. The IRS doesn't call his home and run the risk of his girlfriend finding out about the outstanding amount he owes. Also, he doesn't want to deal with the IRS himself—he wants to sell insurance. He's afraid he may say something that will damage his case. I'm familiar with negotiating with the IRS and anticipating the documentation they'll require. Clients, as a general rule, want no part of this process. As an attorney, I'm skilled in negotiating, and frequently, I'm able to obtain favorable payment terms as well as releases of levies and liens for my clients.

After Mr. Jones' payment plan is set up, the case doesn't end there. Mr. Jones will begin making his payments on the installment agreement. However, because he's self-employed, he must also start paying estimated tax payments, which is something he hasn't done before. For Mr. Jones not to default on his installment agreement, he must file and pay all future federal income taxes on time. In the event that he owes taxes, which he shouldn't as long as he's making his estimated tax payments, he must pay the full amount due to stay in compliance. Starting over and paying the estimated taxes is usually a challenge for most clients because it's not a process they're used to. However, being able to sleep at night and not having to constantly look over their shoulders worrying about the IRS, make it all worthwhile.

How do you know who's the right person to help you with your IRS matter? Here are some criteria to keep in mind when interviewing a tax professional. First, how long has the professional been practicing? It's important to know that the professional you select has the skills, knowledge and experience that will enable them to get the results you desire.

Second, what's the professional's track record? You only want to hire someone who's successful in handling these types of cases.

Third, does the professional concentrate in IRS problem resolution? Many tax professionals prepare taxes or concentrate in tax planning, but tax resolution is a unique field. You only want to hire a professional who has actual training and concentrates only in that field.

Fourth, is the professional's office in your local area? Some tax resolution companies don't have local offices that you can actually meet face to face with the tax professional that you retained. The opportunity to build rapport and the ability to meet face to face with your local tax attorney is priceless.

I've recently had some interesting cases I thought I might share with you. The first couple came into my office in desperation. The IRS was threatening to levy the wife's monthly Social Security Disability payments. The husband had lost his business and was working at a minimum wage job to support their household. This was a couple in their mid-60s who were on the verge of losing everything dear to them—their home and their way of life. The wife was very ill; she had severe depression, and the stress of the IRS coming after them was almost too much for her to cope with.

They retained me to handle all communications with the IRS and negotiate a settlement for the debt they owed. At the time they retained me, they didn't have any outstanding tax returns, but they owed the IRS in excess of $85,000 for four years of unpaid tax returns. Over the next nine months, due to their perilous financial condition, I was able to submit an offer in compromise to the IRS and negotiate a success-ful total payoff of $9,000. They've now finished paying their offer in compromise completely, and the IRS has released the lien against their home. They're thrilled that they can get back to concentrating on what's important to them: her health and paying their bills. I received a very nice thank you letter from them which stated that when they received the Certificate of Release of Federal Tax Lien, it was one of the corner-stones of returning them to a new start at life.

Another client was a man who had gotten behind in his self-employ-ment tax payments and ended up owing the IRS more than $35,000. The IRS had been sending him reminder letters for about three years, which he'd been ignoring. However, because the IRS had become much more threatening in their tone, he decided he needed to address the situation. He'd also been ill over the past few years, with a series of fairly serious medical issues. As a result, he had significant medical bills that weren't covered by his health insurance. I performed a financial analysis on him and determined that he would be an excellent candidate for an offer in compromise. When I was ready to submit the offer package, his finan-cial situation became even worse as his hours at his job were reduced. During the process of negotiating his offer with the IRS, he became ill again and was hospitalized for several months. Due to the fact that his financial situation was so dire, I was able to obtain an offer in compro-mise for him in the amount of $1,600. Because of his significant medi-cal bills he was now going to have to pay and his reduced hours at his job, he was overjoyed with the amount of the offer in compromise, as he was able to pay it and resolve his issue with the IRS in a short amount of time.

Please keep in mind that these results don't happen every time, and these clients had very unfortunate financial situations. However, clearly, the best time to negotiate with the IRS is when a client's financial situ-ation is the most dire. The clients who understand that important point are the ones who are able to work with me to obtain the best result.

As I stated earlier, many of my clients get into IRS trouble not for some nefarious reason but because they had some traumatic event happen to them that snowballed out of control. They're not able to deal with all of life's daily incidents, and they have to let some things slide. Usually, that means the IRS, whether it's not filing their tax returns, not paying their estimated taxes, or not paying their yearly federal taxes. Until that revenue officer knocks on their front door, tows their car away or levies their wages, the IRS just doesn't become the next crisis that they have to deal with.

About Mary

Mary's career as an attorney began in 1993 after graduating from Stetson University College of Law. She graduated from the University of Florida with a Bachelor of Science in Business Administration in 1988 and a Master of Business Administration in Finance from Wake Forest University, Babcock Graduate School of Management, in 1990. Mary was a founding member of the recolonized chapter of Sigma Kappa Sorority, Beta Tau Chapter, at the University of Florida. Her career in law has primarily focused on representing individuals and businesses that have IRS tax problems, ranging from unfiled tax returns to audits.

Mary is a member of the Florida Bar and licensed to practice in the U.S. District Court, Middle District of Florida and the U.S. Tax Court. She's a member of the American Business Women's Association—Sunrise Chapter, the Sarasota County Bar Association, and the Sarasota Area Alumnae Chapter of Sigma Kappa Sorority. As a native Floridian, she grew up in St. Petersburg and has lived in Sarasota since 1999 with her husband Steve and their two black Labrador Retrievers.

Mary is a frequent guest speaker for civic organizations. On several occasions, she has also been a guest columnist for the Sarasota County Bar Association's monthly newspaper, *The Docket*. Mary has been interviewed for the *Bradenton Herald* as well as numerous radio stations in the Sarasota area concerning her knowledge of IRS issues.

To learn more about Mary and how she can help you or your business resolve your IRS tax problems, please visit her website at taxlawyerflorida.com, or contact her for a free consultation at (877) SOS-TAX-LAW.

CHAPTER 4

Compliance Is Key to Limiting Your Potential Tax Liabilities

By Yael N. Lazar, Esq.

I've always believed that knowledge is power, which is why I spend a great deal of time educating my clients. We live in a time where individuals are fighting back against big business and too much government, when we as a society feel helpless and fearful of dealing with the IRS. I'm writing this chapter to help you protect your financial life from the IRS and give you control by empowering you and keeping you from making costly mistakes. I can't tell you how many times I've heard from clients "I didn't know that, my accountant never told me that, or I wished I had known that, then I would have handled it differently." I hope that the knowledge I'm about to share with you will eliminate some of your fears. If you understand what the IRS wants and how it wants it, you can protect yourself from your tax liabilities growing to the point where your interest and penalties are more than your underlying tax liability.

My typical client is generally someone who prepares their return or has it prepared by a professional. They realize that they owe taxes for various reasons, but they don't have the financial ability to pay what they owe at that time. Therefore, they mistakenly believe that if they don't file their return by April 15, the IRS doesn't yet know that they owe the tax. They believe they've bought themselves extra time to save up the money to pay their liability. The problem with this scenario is that life generally gets in the way. They never really save up the money, they don't file the return, and before they know it, it's time to file the next year's return, and so the problem snowballs. Does this sound like you or someone you know? You're not alone!

Many tax payers are unaware that failure to file their tax returns is a criminal offense. In fact, it's a misdemeanor punishable by up to one year in federal prison for every return not filed. If you think that taxpayers don't go to federal prison for failing to file a return, I have a few clients I could introduce you to. They'll tell you a very different story.

If you fail to file a tax return, after a certain period of time, the IRS will graciously file one on your behalf called a "substitute for return," or "SFR." This return will be prepared by the IRS according to all the income that was reported to them on your behalf without any additional exemptions or expenses you may be entitled to. Therefore, the liability established by the "SFR" is most often greater than the actual liability owed. Furthermore, the IRS won't grant you an installment agreement based on SFRs. You must file your own return to replace the SFR filed on your behalf.

Another important reason to file on time is that the IRS only has 10 years to collect the taxes you owe. That 10-year clock starts ticking from the time your tax return is filed and the tax is assessed. How does this work? If you filed your 2000 tax return on time in April 2001, your tax liability would expire in 2011, and the IRS could no longer collect from you. However, if you didn't file your 2000 tax return until October 2005, the IRS would be able to collect from you until October 2015.

Although it's a crime to not file your tax return, not having the money to pay your taxes is *not* a criminal offense. The IRS is looking for that tax return by April 15 of every year or by October 15, if you filed an extension. However, if you filed an extension, that's only an extension of time to file the return. It's not an extension of time to pay the tax due. Any tax due must be paid by April 15, along with your extension. This is very important in terms of limiting your tax liability because you'll be charged interest on that outstanding balance retroactively from April 15. Additionally, you'll also be charged with the failure-to-pay penalty. I'll discuss this penalty later in the chapter.

FAILURE-TO-FILE PENALTY

If you fail to file your return, you'll be charged with the failure-to-file penalty. This penalty is 5 percent per month of the unpaid taxes for each month or part of a month that your return is late. This penalty won't exceed 25 percent of your unpaid taxes. The bottom line is if your return is five or more months late, you'll be paying a 25 percent penalty. To put numbers to this, if you owed $10,000 in taxes, just by not filing your return on time, you'd owe $2,500 in a failure-to-file penalty. If you already had difficulty paying the $10,000 in taxes, can you imagine having to come up with an additional $2,500 just because you failed to file your return on time? If you file your return more than 60 days after the due date or extended due date, the minimum penalty is the smaller of $135 or 100 percent of the unpaid tax.

The failure-to-file penalty is generally more than the failure-to-pay penalty. So if you can't pay all the taxes you owe, you should still file your tax return on time and explore other payment options in the meantime. The IRS will work with you. Compliance with filing requirements is also very important because the IRS won't grant you an installment agreement to pay off your liabilities or any other resolution options if you have any unfiled returns.

FAILURE-TO-PAY PENALTY

If you don't pay your taxes by the due date, you'll generally get hit with a failure-to-pay penalty of one-half of 1 percent of your unpaid taxes for each month or part of a month after the due date that the taxes aren't paid. This penalty can be as much as 25 percent of your unpaid taxes. If you filed a request for an extension to file on time, and you paid at least 90 percent of your actual tax liability by the original due date, you won't be faced with a failure-to-pay penalty if the remaining balance is paid by the extended due date. If both the failure-to-file penalty and the failure-to-pay penalty apply in any month, the 5 percent failure-to-file penalty is reduced by the failure-to-pay penalty. However, if you file your return more than 60 days after the due date or extended due date, the minimum penalty is the smaller of $135 or 100 percent of the unpaid tax. For taxpayers who filed on time, the failure-to-pay penalty rate is reduced to one-quarter of 1 percent per month during any month in which the taxpayer has a valid installment agreement in force.

PENALTY ABATEMENT

If you can show the IRS that you failed to file or pay your taxes on time because of reasonable cause and not because of willful neglect, you won't have to pay a failure-to-file or failure-to-pay penalty. Examples of reasonable cause include loss of employment, illness or caring for a sick loved one, etc. The IRS will remove the penalties charged to your account as well as the interest that has accrued on these penalties.

ESTIMATED TAX-RELATED PENALTIES

Employees have taxes withheld from their paychecks by their employer. When you have income that's not subject to withholding, you may have to make estimated tax payments during the year. This usually applies to individuals who are self-employed. It also includes, but is not limited to, income derived from interest, dividends, rent, alimony, prizes and awards. You should also pay estimated taxes if the amount being withheld from your wages, pension or other income isn't enough to pay your tax liability. Many of my clients have fallen into this trap. For example, a married client with two children should claim four or less exemptions on his W-4 form to insure the proper tax amount is being withheld. Unfortunately, as a result of our current economic times, I've had clients claim upward of 7 to 10 exemptions to maximize the amount of their paycheck to make ends meet each month. The problem is that you're just robbing Peter to pay Paul. You may end up having more money to pay your monthly bills, but come April 15, you would have under-withheld, which means not only do you owe money for taxes, but it's likely you won't have the funds to pay the IRS, and you'll get hit with the additional penalties to add insult to injury.

Estimated tax payments are used to pay income tax and self-employment tax, as well as other taxes and amounts reported on your tax return. If you don't pay enough through withholding or estimated tax payments, you may have to pay a penalty. If you don't pay enough by the due date of each payment period, you may be charged a penalty, even if you're due a refund when you file your tax return.

ACCURACY-RELATED PENALTIES

There are two types of accuracy-related penalties. There's the "substantial understatement" penalty and the "negligence or disregard of the rules or regulations" penalty. These penalties are calculated as a flat 20 percent of the net tax understatement.

1. *Substantial understatement:* You understate your tax if the tax shown on your return is less than the correct tax. The understatement is substantial if it's more than the larger of 10 percent of the correct tax, or $5,000 for individuals.

2. *Negligence and disregard of the rules and regulations*: According to the IRS, "negligence" includes (but is not limited to) any failure to:
   - make a reasonable attempt to comply with the internal revenue laws
   - exercise ordinary and reasonable care in preparation of a tax return
   - keep adequate books and records or to substantiate items properly

This penalty may be asserted if you carelessly, recklessly or intentionally disregard IRS rules and regulations by taking a position on your return with little or no effort to determine whether it's correct or knowingly taking a position that's incorrect. You won't have to pay a negligence penalty if there was a reasonable cause for a position you took, and you acted in good faith.

CIVIL FRAUD PENALTY

If the IRS determines there's any underpayment of tax on your return due to fraud, a penalty of 75 percent will be added to your tax. The fraud penalty on a joint return doesn't apply to a spouse, unless some part of the underpayment is due to the spouse. Negligence or ignorance of the law doesn't constitute fraud.

Typically, IRS examiners who find substantial evidence of fraud will refer the case to the IRS Criminal Investigation Division for potential criminal prosecution. It's important for you to understand that both civil sanctions and criminal prosecution may be imposed. For example, you'll get hit with a civil fraud penalty if you're a "tax protestor" and believe you don't have to file returns and pay taxes like the rest of us or if you've fallen prey to a scam that provides a huge undeserved refund.

FRIVOLOUS TAX RETURN PENALTY

If you choose to file a frivolous tax return or other frivolous submissions, you may have to pay a penalty of $5,000. If you jointly file a frivolous tax return with your spouse, both you and your spouse may each have to pay a penalty of $5,000. A frivolous tax return is one that doesn't include enough information to figure the correct tax or that contains information clearly showing that the tax you reported is substantially incorrect.

You'll have to pay the penalty if you filed this kind of return or submission based on a frivolous position or a desire to delay or interfere with the administration of federal tax laws. According to the IRS, this includes altering or striking out the preprinted language above the space provided for your signature. Tax protestors fall into this category as well.

I hope it's now perfectly clear to you the importance of filing your tax return on time and accurately each year, and how costly it can be if you don't. If you don't have the ability to pay your tax liability in full, don't worry. The IRS will give you a low-interest loan (currently 3 percent) to pay it off. That's a much lower rate than any of your credit card balances!

About Yael

Yael N. Lazar, Esq., also known as the "IRS Angel," is a tax attorney in Garden City, New York. Yael is a tax resolution expert that's regularly sought out by individuals and businesses with income tax, employment tax and civil penalty liabilities on the IRS and state level.

Yael works out a reasonable course of action and overall strategy her clients can live with, which often produces results well beyond their expectations, but, most important, restores her clients' ability to sleep peacefully without the stress and fear of uncertainty.

Yael is the author of *Help for Your IRS Problems* and was recently nominated by the Long Island Press "Best of Long Island for 2012" in the lawyer and law firm category, and was voted "Best of Long Island for 2012" in the lawyer category. Yael has been seen on the Cablevision Channel 18 show "The Hot Seat," and has been heard many times on the Ed Linzer "Give Yourself Credit" radio show on WNYH 740am, the Ken Landau show "Law You Should Know" on WHPC 90.3FM, and "Plugged into Long Island" on WBAB 102.3FM. She has also appeared on "Meet the Experts," which aired on ABC, CBS, NBC and FOX affiliates.

Yael is a member of the New York Bar, U.S. Tax Court, Federal Court for the Eastern and Southern Districts. She holds a J.D. from Saint John's University School of Law and a B.A. from SUNY at Stony Brook where she graduated Phi Beta Kappa and Magna Cum Laude. She's also the founder and chair of Angels for Austin, a nonprofit organization that helps children suffering from Landau-Kleffner Syndrome. She spends her spare time sailing and snowboarding with her husband, Bill, and their three children, Taylor, Kyra and Catie.

To learn more about Yael N. Lazar, Esq., the IRS Angel, and how you can learn the "3 things you should never tell the IRS," visit www.irsangel.com or call toll-free (888)694-7743. For consultations, call (516) 683-1313.

CHAPTER 5

Selecting an ALLSTAR Tax Resolution Team

By John P. Willis, IV

When the IRS comes knocking at your door, how will you answer? Your best response would be to refer the IRS to your tax resolution representative, because when you have IRS issues, you have serious problems. You need a reputable, trained professional experienced in dealing with the IRS and tax resolution issues in order to achieve the best outcome possible. Learn what to look for in a tax resolution representative or tax resolution firm so you can choose the most appropriate professional to solve your tax problems.

If you have a tax problem, how should you select a tax resolution representative? What type of individual or firm would best serve your needs? What information should you be prepared to provide? What should you look for in terms of fees? It's critical that you hire a seasoned professional who has the knowledge and experience to help you solve your tax problems and guide you in developing a game plan to avoid similar problems in the future.

FINDING A REPUTABLE TAX
RESOLUTION PROFESSIONAL

Over the past several years there has been a tremendous shakeup in the tax relief industry. Many of the large national advertising companies that claim to be specialists or experts in tax resolution have been investigated and sued by the Federal Trade Commission and numerous states' attorneys general offices for consumer fraud and/or deceptive and unfair trade practices. Class action lawsuits have also been filed by individuals and businesses, alleging consumer fraud. Some of these companies have been shut down by order of the federal courts. Several have filed bankruptcy. Others that actually had attorneys on staff have pending disciplinary proceedings with their respective state bar associations. These proceedings will most likely result in attorneys being disbarred. National television advertising and attractive internet websites can make a company appear impressive, but when you call their toll-free number for a consultation, is your consultation with an attorney or a "sales" associate?

If you're wondering if it matters whether you give your information to an attorney, a Certified Public Accountant (CPA) or another representative, consider this: If you have a medical concern, would you want to talk to the doctor or to someone who took a few medical courses in college? Or to the actor in the doctor's promotional brochure? You'd want the doctor, right? He's fully trained and credentialed and has the tools and experience to treat your medical issues.

When people have IRS issues, they're anxious and stressed, just as they are when they're sick. If you have tax problems and that's how you feel, it's understandable; however, it's not a reason to accept the first "quick fix" you're offered as a solution to your tax problems. Your first step should be to schedule a consultation with a licensed attorney, a CPA or an enrolled agent (an individual who has met specific requirements to represent taxpayers before the IRS). The representative or firm you consider should have an A+ rating with the Better Business Bureau (BBB). That A+ rating will at least tell you that the BBB has given its highest rating to them or their firm.

Some of the large, factory-type tax resolution businesses replace qualified attorneys with salespeople who have little or no tax experience. These salespeople, who answer customer questions and sell their companies' services, promise things they can't deliver just to get the sale. There have even been recent news reports in which sales associates at some national chains have told prospective clients that IRS collection actions will cease as soon as the client contracts with their company and pays the fee. Not true! This may be what you would like to hear, but just signing up with such a company and paying their fee won't put an end to your IRS problems.

WHAT *DOES* A REPUTABLE TAX RESOLUTION PROFESSIONAL DO?

An experienced tax resolution professional must perform very specific actions in order to successfully engage the IRS on your behalf. An attorney, a CPA or an enrolled agent who's a reputable tax resolution professional should begin with some serious fact-finding. Often, an initial consultation can take an hour or longer to collect the complete information on existing tax issues. It's important to be honest with the tax professional at this consultation. A prospective client who describes a history with the IRS that doesn't accurately reflect all his prior actions or inactions, such as failing to report previous IRS installment agreements on which the taxpayer has defaulted, limits the tax professional's ability to select the best available options for solving that tax problem. Factors such as these can be game changers because they restrict choices for tax resolution in your case with the IRS.

Tax resolution professionals need to know exactly where you stand. Reputable tax professionals expect the taxpayer to be an active participant in the entire process. The taxpayer will be required to collect and provide a significant amount of specific information. Just a few things a tax professional might ask include:

- *Do you owe individual, corporate, payroll, estate or excise taxes?*

- *Do you owe federal or state taxes, or both?*

- *Do you have any unfiled tax returns? If so, what years have returns not been filed?*

- *What are your financial goals?* Most tax firms assume that your only concern is the IRS, but life is often more complicated. An experienced tax professional will help you develop a tax resolution plan that works best for your current tax problems as well as your overall life goals.

- *Do you believe that you overpaid your taxes?* If so, you have a limited amount of time to file a claim for a credit or a refund. Be prepared to list the year(s) and possible tax considerations that might apply.

- *Are you confused and overwhelmed?* If you are, put down on paper what you do know about your current tax problems. Even if you don't know what the IRS wants, a seasoned tax resolution professional will help you discover the nature and extent of your tax problems and will discuss your best options.

QUALIFICATIONS OF A COMPETENT
TAX RESOLUTION REPRESENTATIVE

Experienced tax resolution professionals know your options and are fully aware of the consequences of every statement given to the IRS. Talking directly to someone from the IRS is a stressful experience that can quickly turn into a personal conflict. If you lose your head or say the wrong thing to an IRS employee, or if you provide information beyond what's required, it can be used by the IRS to build its case against you, likely resulting in a negative outcome. More often than not, you could have saved money and avoided the associated stress if you had consulted with a qualified tax resolution professional first, *before* talking to the IRS directly.

Before selecting your tax resolution representative, you should ask the following questions:

- *Are you a licensed attorney, a CPA or an enrolled agent?* These three types of individuals have the appropriate credentials to represent taxpayers before the IRS.

- *Do you regularly participate in tax law and tax resolution continuing education activities?* Continuing education habits reveal how the tax professional stays abreast of changes in tax law and tax resolution.

- *Are you an active member of any professional organization, association or society that's tax resolution-specific?* Active membership in tax resolution-specific professional organizations demonstrates current involvement and interest in the profession.

- *What percentage of your practice is devoted to IRS tax resolution?* A high concentration of tax resolution in a practice speaks to the amount of experience and focus in the tax resolution field. Less than 100 percent translates into less tax resolution experience. It also reflects a focus on other areas of the law.

Many of the questionable tax resolution companies currently advertising on television or on the internet have too few adequately trained or appropriately prepared employees. Your initial consultation regarding tax resolution representation should be with a licensed attorney, a CPA or an enrolled agent. Only someone with their credentials would be qualified to ask the right questions, review your tax-specific information and propose realistic resolution options.

If a tax resolution company only conducts business by telephone, employs high-pressure sales tactics, or requires your credit card or bank account number upfront, expect minimal individualized attention from employees with varying experience and qualifications, and little to no follow-up assistance.

Don't be impressed if a firm claims to have former IRS employees on its staff. These employees don't necessarily provide an inside track when dealing with the IRS. Former IRS employees could be biased toward the IRS and thus poor taxpayer advocates. In fact, former IRS employees often view taxpayers who owe money as guilty until proven innocent!

TAX RESOLUTION FEE STRUCTURE

Choose a tax resolution professional who offers *fixed-fee pricing*, which is a fee charged for a defined scope of professional services to be performed based on your needs. Businesses that don't offer fixed-fee pricing usually either have open-ended fee structures in which they collect an initial retainer fee and then bill their time by the hour or they charge a base fee for a minimal level of service, and then charge separate additional fees for every service that must be added to solve your tax problems.

A reputable tax resolution professional tells a client at the end of their initial consultation what work needs to be performed and outlines the scope of professional services that will be provided for a specific fee.

This is where the fact-finding conducted by a seasoned tax resolution professional proves important. The more thorough and complete the initial consultation and fact-finding, the more accurate the proposed scope of services and proposed fee can be. If the information provided isn't thorough or complete, the proposed scope of services could be inappropriate and the accompanying fee would be insufficient, potentially leading to additional billing or inadequate representation. For example, if a revenue officer (an IRS collections employee from a local field office) is involved in your case, more expedited and additional work must be performed because the IRS has already begun to take an active interest in collecting your tax debt. If the fact that a revenue officer has been assigned to your case isn't revealed in your initial consultation, the scope of services selected won't be sufficient because it won't cover representation with a revenue officer.

GUARANTEED RESULTS—BUYER BEWARE

The reputable tax resolution professional doesn't promise what he can't deliver. A professional with your best interests in mind should spell out several different scenarios that might occur as your case unfolds, offering options and choices along the way. If you're offered guaranteed results after just an initial consultation, you're most likely not dealing with a reliable tax resolution business. A reputable tax resolution professional can't guarantee a specific final result with the IRS any more than a professional quarterback in the NFL can guarantee a win on the football field.

Rather than focusing on promised results, consider whether the tax resolution professional has a solid reputation and is well respected in the community. Referrals from family, friends or other trusted professionals can be very helpful. Additionally, testimonials from previous clients are a good source of information, even though some can be fabricated. These resources provide a great starting point as you begin your search for the right tax resolution professional to successfully resolve your tax issues.

ADVANTAGES TO HIRING AN ATTORNEY

There are significant advantages to hiring the right attorney to help you solve your tax problems. Most people are familiar with the term attorney-client privilege: the specific, defined, privileged relationship between an attorney and client. Unlike other professionals, like CPAs or enrolled agents, an attorney can't be forced to testify against his client in court. An attorney is a trained advocate for his client. CPAs and enrolled agents are not. While a CPA's expertise may be needed to provide the numbers or figures related to your tax issues, CPAs aren't specifically trained to argue a taxpayer's case or to defend a taxpayer before the IRS. While it's true that a CPA or an enrolled agent alone can represent a taxpayer before the IRS, neither is typically the best representative to argue, advocate or advance a taxpayer's position.

DANGEROUS TIME FOR SMALL-BUSINESS OWNERS AND THE SELF-EMPLOYED

Small-business owners and self-employed individuals are especially vulnerable today. The IRS is moving quickly to identify individuals and businesses who owe back taxes and is fairly aggressive in its collection of those back taxes. Understandably, many things can happen in a slow economy. In some cases, business slows down but the business owner keeps employees on the payroll longer than he should because he anticipates business improving. In other cases, accounts receivables have slowed, creating a cash flow deficit. If a small-business owner "borrows" from employee payroll tax withholdings to pay outstanding bills, he's entering dangerous territory. The IRS considers this employee theft, and the penalties are exceedingly high. If the IRS doesn't immediately identify the business's failure to timely deposit the amount owed in payroll taxes, then penalties and interest will be substantial and they'll accrue exponentially by the time the problem is referred to a tax resolution professional.

If you're a small-business owner in this situation, you should ask a tax resolution professional if he's experienced in dealing with payroll tax cases. An answer such as "I can probably do something with it," suggests less than effective payroll tax resolution skills. The correct answer should be concrete and state the tax resolution professional's expertise and experience in managing and resolving payroll tax cases.

DON'T GO IT ALONE

Some taxpayers might think, "What will cost me less? Attempting to get a final tax resolution on my own or paying a tax professional to get a better final resolution with the IRS?" That line of thinking might get you into trouble. Tax resolution professionals provide a broad array of services that may be of greater value to you and your business than simply saving money. Effective tax resolution planning and management can prevent bank levies, wage garnishments, tax lien filings, real and personal property seizures and business closures.

Consider the client who meets with a tax resolution professional, leaves the meeting uncomfortable, and decides to attempt resolution of his tax issues by contacting the IRS without representation. Maybe he contracts with one of the large national tax resolution chains to represent him before the IRS instead. In either case, this client has probably compounded his tax problems and will likely still be left with tax issues to resolve. The reputable tax resolution professional must now attempt to repair the damage done by providing the IRS information that a seasoned tax resolution professional would have advised him not to provide. Without the potential savings benefit that the tax resolution professional's financial planning could have provided, the IRS will typically deem the taxpayer as having a much greater ability to pay.

An experienced, reputable tax resolution professional is knowledgeable about what the IRS can and cannot do. The financial information you provide to the IRS is their roadmap to collections. If you try to handle your tax problems directly, without professional representation, you may unwittingly provide the IRS information they need to move forward with collection action.

Choosing a tax resolution professional is easily one of the most critical decisions you may make in your life. You'll benefit most if you select a reputable, experienced professional who has the appropriate credentials to represent you before the IRS, has an abundance of experience in handling tax resolution cases, offers fixed-fee pricing, and will help you not only with your immediate tax problems but continue providing assistance with your financial planning and management to keep your life in order.

About John

John Willis is the CEO and founding attorney of John P. Willis, IV, PC, the powerhouse firm behind IRSALLSTAR.com. His law firm focuses exclusively on helping individual taxpayers and businesses solve serious tax problems. The firm is committed to providing each and every client the highest possible level of professional service, legal protection and personal attention.

John founded his law firm in 2002 with the vision of providing excellent, results-driven representation in a relaxed, casual environment. His championship team of experienced tax professionals strives to achieve one goal: tax resolution that produces the best possible outcome for each client. The IRSALLSTAR team has developed a winning formula to ensure that each client's individual needs are specifically met. Upon becoming a client of John's law firm, that client's immediate needs are assessed and long-term goals are defined. Experienced professionals on the IRSALLSTAR team then assist each client in developing and implementing a custom-tailored game plan to provide both short- and long-term relief from his or her serious tax problems. All firm clients are continually coached toward successful tax resolution and final victory over their challenges with the IRS and state taxing authorities.

John believes strongly in supporting and representing the "underdog" and has devoted his entire professional life to protecting and defending those who need it most. As an attorney, John takes his role as "counselor" seriously. His knowledge, creativity and persistence are valuable assets that provide substantial benefits to his clients. He has represented individuals and businesses across the Gulf Coast for more than 14 years, and he brings together an abundance of skills and experience that can be of assistance to almost anyone. John has been featured as one of America's Premier Tax Professionals in USA Today and seen on ABC, NBC, CBS and FOX affiliates around the country.

Born and raised in New Orleans, John currently lives in Daphne, Alabama, on the Eastern Shore of Mobile Bay. He's admitted to practice before the U.S. Tax Court and can represent taxpayers from anywhere in the United States before the IRS. John is a member of the Alabama State Bar and the Florida Bar, and he's admitted to practice before the U.S. Courts of Appeal for the 6th and 11th Circuits and the U.S. District Courts for the Middle and Northern Districts of Alabama. Additionally, he's an active member of the American Society of Tax Problem Solvers.

John's law firm, John P. Willis, IV, PC, is located in the heart of downtown Fairhope, Alabama, and represents clients from across the southeastern United States.

To learn more about John and his law firm, visit www.IRSALLSTAR.com or call toll-free (877) 254-4254.

CHAPTER 6

How to Protect Against Losing Your Business to the IRS

By Jeffrey T. Jones

Joe and Laura owned their own moderately successful business. Joe was the president and Laura the secretary. Joe did the work, Laura kept the books, and they had six employees.

For years, they had made all their 941/payroll tax payments without a problem. Then the economy got tight and business slacked off. Their customers either couldn't pay their bills or could only pay part of them.

The end of the business tax quarter came. They looked at their bank account, and they owed their suppliers, employees and the IRS. There was only enough money to pay either the IRS or their suppliers and employees.

They thought, "Well, if we don't pay suppliers and employees, we won't have a business at all. The IRS won't miss this, and we'll make it up next quarter." The next quarter came and business had picked up some, so they were able to pay all the bills and that quarter's 941 payment, but they weren't able to make up last quarter's payment. Instead, they decided they'd do it next time.

The following month, they had an excellent month, and they made a lot of money. They were happy and invested some of the money back into the business and took a nice paycheck for themselves. The next month business was down, and so was the month after that. It came to the end of the quarter, and they looked at the bank statement and wondered where all the money had gone. Again, they had a choice: "Well, the IRS didn't miss it the last time we didn't pay it, so they won't miss this time!" So once again they paid suppliers and employees.

This went on for several more months. Sometimes they could pay the 941taxes; other times they couldn't. Finally, it got to the point where they had to start laying of workers. They laid off half their workers and were behind on paying their suppliers. They stopped making all 941 payments, and they began getting letters from the IRS. They opened the first letter, then began ignoring the rest. One day there was a knock on the door: "Hi, I'm from the IRS, and we're here to shut your business down."

Sound too incredible to be true? Think again. This happens all over the United States every day, and it could happen to you if you don't keep current on your payroll taxes.

The IRS is very diligent about collecting payroll taxes. It's nothing for them to shut down your business and liquidate your assets in order to collect the taxes owed. They have special powers granted to them by the U.S. Government to go into your bank account and take your money, along with seizing your house, Social Security benefits, 401Ks, IRAs, accounts receivable, you name it! Anything of value that can pay off the debt, they can seize.

Payroll taxes can't be discharged in bankruptcy and not paying payroll taxes can be considered a federal crime, if the IRS can prove you "willfully" failed to pay.

What are payroll taxes? Well, they're referred to as Trust Fund taxes, because basically, you, the employer, have been entrusted with money belonging to your employees. It's your job to withhold a portion of the money from employees to pay their income tax and their share of FICA/ Social Security and Medicare. So, in reality, it's not your money. It's taxes that are due to the United States. You're just the one responsible for delivering it to them. If you don't pay it, it's considered theft.

If you're found to be a person "responsible" for paying the payroll taxes and you don't pay them, the IRS will eventually assess the Trust Fund Recovery Penalty (TFRP) against you personally. The TFRP is the portion of the employees' payroll taxes you didn't pay.

In Joe and Laura's case, both would be considered responsible parties under the IRS criteria:

1. Did the person have a duty to account for, collect and pay the payroll taxes, and

2. Did they willfully fail to perform that duty?

Joe and Laura didn't intentionally defraud the United States by not paying the 941taxes. They, like most people with these problems, have "too much month at the end of the money." In other words, things get tight and what little money you have, you want to use to keep the business open, so you pay bills, suppliers and yourself by lending yourself the employee's payroll taxes.

Your intention is always to pay it back. You tell yourself it's just a short-term loan. But it's a terrible loan, because by not paying on time, you not only have to come up with the money later but also money for penalties for not paying and for not filing the 941 return. Plus, there will be interest on top of that.

Once the IRS gets wind of you, this is what will happen: First, you'll get notices demanding that you pay the taxes, plus the penalties and interest. If you still don't pay after that, the IRS will next determine the people or persons who are responsible for paying the taxes. They'll schedule an interview with you, and once you get the notice, you'll have only 60 days to prepare for the interview. During the interview, they'll question you, among other things, about the following:

• Who can sign the checks?

• Who guarantees and co-signs loans?

• Who prepares, signs and/or reviews the 941 returns and makes the payments?

• Who has the authority to authorize payroll and to decide what bills get paid?

• Were any financial obligations paid during the time the 941's were not paid?

- Who has the authority to hire and fire?

- What banks do you use and who's on the signature cards?

- When did you become aware taxes were owed and what did you do about it?

What they're trying to determine is the person(s) responsible for paying the payroll taxes. The IRS wants to find as many responsible persons as they can. It makes the likelihood of collecting the taxes greater.

In Joe and Laura's situation, it's probable that they would both be held to be responsible persons because they were both officers in the business, signed checks, reviewed the 941 returns, decided to pay other financial obligations other than the IRS, and were aware they owed the tax and didn't pay it.

Now, let's put a twist on this. Let's assume that Laura isn't married to Joe and isn't an officer in the business. She's just an employee who does the taxes, writes the checks, fills out the 941 returns, and knows the taxes should be paid but is told by Joe not to pay them, and to pay other financial obligations instead. Would Laura then be considered a responsible person? I'm sure most people would say "no, she is just an employee and is doing what the boss tells her to do. If she doesn't listen to him, she would lose her job. She has no choice."

Guess what? Most people would be *wrong!* In most instances, Laura would be considered a responsible person, and the IRS would come after her, too, for the TFRP. "Wait a minute," you say, "that doesn't make sense. She's an employee. What can she do?"

According to the IRS, she should have quit her job when she was instructed not to pay the payroll taxes that she knew should have been paid. That's right, *quit her job!* That's how serious the IRS takes nonpayment of payroll taxes.

After the responsible person interview is over, the IRS will require you to sign the form, under oath, that all the answers are true. If not, you could face perjury charges. So please don't try to fudge or give half truths, because the IRS will investigate all your answers.

You need to be very careful, because the IRS is very skilled at getting you, or others associated with the business, to say things that will make *you* a responsible person. Their job is to identify you as a target.

If it's determined that you're a responsible person, you'll receive a letter from the IRS telling you that they're assessing you with the TFRP. This is the amount of the employee's taxes you didn't pay! (Remember, this doesn't include the business's half of the delinquent taxes owed.)

After you've been notified that the TFRP has been assessed against you, you only have a limited time to mount a defense and appeal the ruling. If you don't, then the levies against your bank accounts, accounts receivable, and liens against your property will start and can also lead to liquidating your business to get the payments and/or taking any personal tax refunds you're due.

What can you do to stop this? Well, first of all, you need to file any 941 returns that haven't been filed. (*Tip*: Even if you can't pay the 941 taxes, always file the return to help avoid paying the failure-to-file penalty.) Second, get current on your payroll tax deposits. Sometimes it is easier to file the deposits monthly, when you have the money, rather than every quarter. Doing these two things will show the IRS that you want to take care of the problem and become compliant.

Once you've done that, and it looks like you can stay in business, here are the ways to take care of the tax debt:

- *Pay all the taxes, penalties and interest off.* If you're in this situation, this is probably not realistic, but some businesses have been able to do this by getting a big account or selling off assets.

- *Request a Penalty Abatement.* Sometimes penalties can be fully or partially removed depending on the reason or circumstances for non-payment. This won't take away the full amount owed but could greatly reduce it.

- *Enter into an Installment Agreement.* This can only happen if you get current on your 941 payments and tax return filings. Remember, even if you enter into an Installment Agreement, the penalties and interest keep accruing.

- *Request an Offer of Compromise.* This is the famous "pennies on the dollar" settlement that everyone has heard about. It's very difficult to get the IRS to accept one of these. For them to even consider an Offer of Compromise, the business has to be up to date on paying all it's taxes and filing all it's returns for the last two years.

- *Be declared non-collectible.* This means that neither you nor your business has any assets to pay off the debt. Even though you're in non-collectible status, the interest and penalties keep accruing, and the IRS will check back on you periodically to see if you have the financial resources to pay the debt.

- *Call the Taxpayer Advocate Service.* This is an independent office in the IRS that helps individuals and businesses resolve problems with the IRS, but in order to get help, you must prove that you're suffering, or are about to suffer, economic harm.

- *Declare bankruptcy.* While payroll taxes *cannot* be discharged in bankruptcy, bankruptcy may allow some of the other financial pressures to ease up and let you focus on your IRS problem.

- *Try to convince the IRS that, if they shut you down, they'll never get any money because the chances of you getting a high-paying job to pay off the debt are slim.* A lot of this depends on the IRS agent you're dealing with. If it's someone local, they may be more understanding than an agent in another state who doesn't understand the local economy and job situation or that you're the largest employer in a small town and, that if they shut you down, how it would devastate the town.

- *Finally, you need to decide if the business is viable.* We all hate to fail, and sometimes our ego gets in the way. So we try to do everything we can to keep this from happening. This includes making bad business and financial choices, hoping to keep a bad business open, when in our heart we know there's no way to make it work. Sometimes shutting the business down is the best thing to do. It doesn't make sense to keep owing more and more money, when there's no chance to ever pay it off. Many of this country's richest men have shut down failing businesses at some point in their lives. Sometimes the simplest thing to do is start over. Never look at it as a failure; look at it as a bad result you can learn from.

So you see, there *are* ways to solve your tax problems and keep the IRS from shutting your business down. While owing payroll taxes or being assessed the TFRP is no fun and it can wreak havoc on a business and cause you many sleepless nights, there's light at the end of the tunnel. The best thing to do is always make sure you pay the taxes. However, if you get into this situation, call a local tax attorney or tax professional who works with the IRS for advice. He can tell you what needs to be done and guide you in a direction that's best for you and your business.

About Jeff

Jeffrey T. Jones is an attorney in Charleston, West Virginia. He's licensed to practice in the State and Federal Courts of West Virginia and in the State of North Carolina. He's a graduate of the West Virginia University College of Law.

In his practice, he helps individuals and businesses solve their IRS problems. Whether it's back taxes owed, liens, levies, wage garnishments, penalties and interest, payroll or business taxes, Jeff gives each client the individual attention they need to help solve their problem.

Jeff has appeared in *USA Today* as an Emerging Business Leader to Watch and was asked by the IRS to speak on behalf of taxpayers and their representatives at an IRS-sponsored seminar.

He's the author of the book *Dealing With an IRS Problem* and has written special reports dealing with business payroll taxes and ways to solve your IRS problems.

Jeff is past president of the West Virginia Association for Justice and has been honored as Member of the Year. He's also been recognized as one of the Top 100 Trial Lawyers in West Virginia.

He also represents persons injured or killed in car accidents and has written the *West Virginia Automobile Accident Injury Guide* and a special report dealing with car accidents, personal injury and insurance companies.

To learn more about Jeff or to order his book, guide or special reports, go to www.jeffreytjones.com or call (800) 247-2845 or (304) 345-3400.

CHAPTER 7

Free and Clear: Release Your Tax Debt With an Offer in Compromise

By Jim Gilland

Offer in Compromise (or OIC) is an IRS program that allows qualified individuals or businesses with an unpaid tax debt to negotiate a settled amount that's less than the total owed to clear the debt. This includes all taxes, interest, penalties, or additional amounts. The objective of the OIC program is to accept a compromise when it's in the best interests of both the taxpayer and the government, and promotes voluntary compliance with all future payment and filing requirements.

The IRS will accept an offer in compromise when it's unlikely that the tax liability can be collected in full and the amount offered reasonably reflects collection potential. An offer in compromise is a legitimate alternative to declaring a case currently not collectible or to a protracted installment agreement. The goal of the IRS is to achieve collection of what's potentially collectible at the earliest possible time and at the least cost to the government.

ELIGIBILITY

Before a tax payer submits an OIC, they must: 1) file all tax returns they're legally required to file, 2) make all estimated tax payments for the current year, and 3) make all required federal tax deposits for the current quarter if they're a business owner with employees.

Additionally, if you or your business is currently in an open bankruptcy proceeding, you aren't eligible to apply for an offer. Any resolution of your outstanding tax debts generally must take place within the context of your bankruptcy proceeding. If, however, a tax is still outstanding after the bankruptcy is either discharged or dismissed, it may be done at that time.

QUALIFYING CONDITIONS

At least one of three conditions must be met to qualify a taxpayer for consideration of an OIC settlement. These include: Doubt as to Liability, Doubt as to Collectability, and Effective Tax Administration.

Doubt as to Liability

Grounds for compromise may exist when there's a legitimate doubt from the viewpoints of both the taxpayer and the IRS that an assessed tax liability is correct. The taxpayer must argue why he or she isn't liable and provide supporting evidence. The available evidence for both parties is then weighed by the IRS to determine if they agree that at least there's an issue as to whether the assessed tax is correct, thus allowing the IRS to consider accepting a compromised amount.

Doubt as to Collectability

Doubt as to Collectability is the most common approach. Here the debtor must be able to show that the debt is likely uncollectable in full by the IRS under any circumstances. Under this qualifying condition, the IRS will consider a settlement based on the following formula:

Settlement Amount = (monthly disposable income)(x months)
+ the net realizable equity in the taxpayer's assets

Disposable income is monthly income minus allowable monthly expenses. It's important to recognize that the IRS won't allow all expenses that you may actually have. Common disallowed expenses are college tuition payments for a dependent and credit card payments. In general, unsecured debt is disallowed. Additionally, charitable donations are disallowed.

In the formula above, "x" represents the number of months. The number of months over which disposable income must be calculated into the offer amount is based on the smaller of the number of months remaining until the Collection Statute Expiration Date (CSED) for the tax debt or either 48 or 60 months, depending on the payment option for the OIC the applicant is selecting. Forty-eight is used where a lump-sum payment is anticipated; sixty months is used when a payment plan is intended.

Net realizable equity in assets is the quick sale value of the asset. Normally, that is 80 percent of fair market value (FMV) minus any amounts that are secured by the asset (e.g., a car or house). As an example, if a taxpayer has a home worth $100,000 and owes $50,000 on the home, the IRS will calculate the net realizable equity in the asset as follows: ($100,000 x .80) - $50,000 = $30,000. The IRS expects, in this example, that at least the $30,000 will be included in the OIC amount.

If a taxpayer believes he or she qualifies, the taxpayer completes a financial statement on a form provided by the IRS. Wage earners and self-employed individuals use Form 433-A. Form 433-B is for offers involving all other business types. These financial statements identify all assets and liabilities as well as disposable income.

Effective Tax Administration
Under this condition, the debtor doesn't contest liability or collectability but can demonstrate extenuating or special circumstances that the collection of the debt would "create an economic hardship or would be unfair and inequitable." This OIC program is available for any taxpayer but is primarily used by individuals who are elderly, disabled, or have other special extenuating circumstances.

PARTIAL PAYMENT

Effective July 15, 2006, the IRS made changes to the OIC program requiring that 20 percent of the offer amount be paid upfront. This amount is non-refundable but is applied against the tax liability. At the same time an application fee of $150 must be submitted.

There are two exceptions to this rule: First, if the OIC is based solely on doubt as to liability, the application fee isn't required. Second, if an individual (not a corporation, etc.) certifies that their total monthly income meets poverty guidelines established by the U.S. Department of Health and Human Services (contained in Section 4 of Form 656) by filing Form 656A, they're exempted from paying the fee as well as the 20 percent upfront amount.

An offer submitted without the required fees is subject to rejection without appeal. Additionally, if the IRS determines that an individual wasn't exempt from paying the fee, the OIC will be returned without further consideration.

After the IRS receives the offer, the IRS has up to two years to make a decision. If the decision isn't reached by that time, the offer is automatically accepted.

Under the Tax Increase Prevention and Reconciliation Act of 2005 (TIP-RA 2005), if a taxpayer offers to make monthly payments over time, the taxpayer must include with the offer the first month's payment. In this case, the taxpayer isn't required to submit the 20 percent, which applies only to the lump-sum payment option. Then, during the time the offer is being considered by the IRS, the taxpayer must keep making the monthly payments to keep the offer current. If the taxpayer fails to make a payment, the offer will be returned to the taxpayer.

Payment Options

At this writing, there are three types of OIC payment terms that the IRS and the taxpayer may agree to:

1. *Lump Sum Cash:* offer must be paid within five or fewer installments from notice of acceptance[1]

2. *Short Term Periodic Payment:* offer must be paid within 24 months (two years) from the date the IRS receives the OIC

3. *Deferred Periodic Payment:* offer must be paid within 25 months or longer but within the time remaining on the 10-year period for collection

---

1 Author has been able to negotiate with the IRS to allow three months between each of the five payments in some cases.

66

UNDERSTANDING THE PROCESS

It's important to understand what actions the IRS and the debtor may take, or are required to take, throughout the OIC process. This includes while the OIC is being evaluated, if the OIC is accepted, and if the OIC is rejected.

While the OIC is Being Evaluated

While the OIC is being evaluated, the IRS will apply the debtor's non-refundable payments and fees (discussed above under *Partial Payment*) to the tax liability (you may designate payments to a specific tax year and portion of the debt). The IRS may still file a Notice of Federal Tax Lien, although other collection activities are suspended. The legal assessment and collection statute of limitations period is also extended. The debtor must continue to make all required payments associated with the offer but isn't required to make payments on an existing installment

agreement. Additionally, an OIC is automatically accepted if the IRS doesn't make a determination within two years of the IRS receipt date, a good reason to send the offer by certified mail, return receipt requested.

If the OIC Is Accepted

After an OIC has been accepted, the debtor must meet all of the Offer Terms listed in Section 8 of Form 656, including filing all required tax returns on time and making all payments on time. Acceptance of an OIC also means that any refunds due within the calendar year in which the offer is accepted will be applied to the debtor's tax debt—a good reason to carefully evaluate the number of exemptions claimed on the employer's Form W-4.

An OIC will have no effect upon a tax lien. The lien will remain in effect until the offer is accepted by the IRS *and* the full amount of the offer has been paid in full. Once the offered amount has been paid, the taxpayer should request that the IRS remove the lien.

An OIC will stop tax levies under § 301.7122(g)(1) of the U.S. Federal Tax Regulations. That regulation states that the IRS won't levy upon a taxpayer's property while a valid OIC (an offer that has been accepted for processing) is pending and, if rejected, for 30 days after the rejection. If the taxpayer appeals the rejection, the IRS cannot levy while the appeals process is ongoing. If a levy is in place when the offer is submitted, it is not automatically released, however, it may be released upon request.

If the OIC Is Rejected

If the IRS revokes your OIC, the full amount of your tax liability, add on penalties and interest, and potentially aggressive collection efforts can be reinstated. The debtor may appeal the rejection within 30 days using Request for Appeal of Offer in Compromise, Form 13711. It should be noted that in 2004, the IRS approved 19,546 offers, about 16 percent of the total number of offers received. As of May 2010, the IRS has accepted about 24 percent of offers.[2]

NEW STREAMLINED PROCESS

The IRS recently announced new steps to assist struggling taxpayers. These steps include expanding the streamlined OIC program to cover a larger group of struggling taxpayers.

The expanded Streamlined OIC program includes fewer requests for additional financial information, asking for additional information (when necessary) by phone instead of by mail, and greater flexibility when considering taxpayers' ability to pay.

To qualify under this program a taxpayer must either be a wage earner, unemployed, or a self-employed taxpayer with no employees and gross receipts under $500,000. Additionally, total household income must be $100,000 or less, and the amount owed must be less than $50,000 when the OIC offer is filed. Prior to this new step by the IRS, the amount had to be less than $25,000.

CONSUMER ALERT

In September 2011, the IRS reissued a consumer alert advising taxpayers to beware of promoters' claims that tax debts can be settled for "pennies on the dollar" through the OIC program.

According to the IRS, some promoters are inappropriately advising indebted taxpayers to file an OIC application with the IRS, even when the taxpayers clearly don't qualify. This bad advice costs taxpayers money and time. This author is aware, through IRS sources, that the largest "pennies on the dollar" promoter, who coincidentally recently filed a

2 National Taxpayer Advocate, 2011 Objectives Report to Congress

Chapter 7 Bankruptcy, submitted offers of $500 on every offer requested. Clearly, they made no effort to determine the proper amount to offer the IRS in each individual case.

IRS Commissioner Mark W. Everson has stated, "This program serves an important purpose for a select group of taxpayers. But we are increasingly concerned about unscrupulous promoters charging excessive fees to taxpayers who have no chance of meeting the program's requirements. We urge taxpayers not to be duped by high-priced promises."

OIC PROGRAM IMPROVEMENTS SHOW LACKLUSTER RESULTS

The IRS OIC program recently came under criticism from within. In their June 2010 report to congress, the National Taxpayer Advocate (NTA), a division of the IRS, pointed out numerous problems with the OIC program.[3] According to the NTA, the underutilization of the OIC program by the IRS directly conflicts with both the IRS' policy statement and Congress' intent for the program. Despite recent IRS initiatives to help taxpayers submit acceptable OICs, such as a second review of home values and guidelines for offers from low-income taxpayers, the number of OICs accepted has shown little improvement. Acceptances declined 72 percent from 2001 to 2009—and this while OIC receipts have continued to increase, 11 percent in the last year alone. The NTA is especially concerned with the Centralized OIC Unit (COIC). While offer dispositions have increased by 22 percent in 2010, 97 percent of this increase in dispositions is attributable to the COIC. Moreover, the number of OIC applications returned to taxpayers increased by 44 percent in FY 2010, with most of the increase attributable to COIC. This has caused the NTA to worry that the COIC is automatically returning offers without having a real conversation with taxpayers.

The NTA is concerned that taxpayers are being significantly harmed by the large increase in returned offers. If the taxpayer submits an offer and it ends up being returned, the taxpayer loses his or her $150 OIC application fee and any partial payments, and doesn't receive any appeal rights to contest the return determination. The NTA concluded that the increased number of returned offers may indicate that taxpayers are

---

3 National Taxpayer Advocate, Objectives Report to Congress for FY 2011, p. 20-22, available at http://www.irs.gov/pub/irs-utl/nta2011objectivesfinal.pdf.

either having difficulty understanding the application process or that OIC employees aren't working with taxpayers to resolve application problems, or both.

It has been noted by the NTA that the OIC program has deep problems. The NTA has also complained that even when dealing with taxpayers in the current troubled economy, the IRS has failed to make the OIC program an integral part of its collection strategy.

While the NTA has applauded recent revised IRS procedures for calculating taxpayers' future income during OIC evaluation, it remains concerned that the revised procedures don't clearly instruct IRS employees to apply flexibility and good judgment when calculating future income.

In particular, the NTA believes the IRS should remind its employees of Policy Statement 5-100, which says, "An offer in compromise is a legitimate alternative to declaring a case currently not collectible or to a protracted installment agreement. The goal is to achieve collection of what is potentially collectible at the earliest possible time and at the least cost to the government." The NTA also believes that to achieve the stated goal of "going the extra mile to help taxpayers," these OIC procedures may need to be completely rewritten.

About Jim

Jim Gilland is a nationally recognized tax attorney whose practice is limited to IRS tax controversy matters. He holds a Juris Doctorate from Drake University Law School in DeMoines, Iowa, a Master of Science from Brigham Young, and a Bachelor of Science from Brigham Young. He has been interviewed on the "Brian Tracy" show and also seen on NBC, CBS, ABC and FOX affiliates, as well as in the *Wall Street Journal, USA Today* and *Newsweek*. He has been quoted by radio personalities for constantly maintaining that "ALL IRS tax problems can be solved." His book, *How to Solve Your IRS Problem!* has been a lifesaver for many taxpayers throughout the United States.

Most IRS problems solved at Gilland Law Firm are accomplished through partial or full-pay installment agreements, Offer In Compromise, obtaining Currently Not Collectible Status, and audit reconsiderations. Some are resolved partially or wholly through bankruptcy. Additionally, strategy and timing are often critical issues to synergize a minimal tax result using one or more of these procedures in conjunction with others. There are multiple other methods to eliminate or lower tax penalties and associated interest.

Jim is an avid cyclist, having raced the longest one-day USCF-sanctioned bike race, LOTOJA, 10 years in a row. The 206-mile race starts in Logan, Utah, winds through Idaho, and finishes in Jackson Hole, Wyoming. He won the race in 2005.

Jim may be contacted at Gilland Law Firm in Salt Lake City at (801) 444-9302; information on solving IRS problems is available at www.utahtaxattorney.pro.

CHAPTER 8

Revenge: The Case of the Hung Mistletoe

By Anthony E. Parent, Esq.

It was the Tuesday before Thanksgiving, and I was getting ready to leave my office for the day. Before I could do so, my firm's Resolution Director, Victoria Currier, called me into her office. She needed my help.

That was odd. Normally she could handle any intake on her own. On the walk back to her office she was agitated. She told me the IRS levied the bank accounts of a prospective client, "Roberta," even though she was in an installment agreement.

On speakerphone, I could hear that Roberta was in tears. She explained that she attempted to speak to the revenue officer's supervisor, but that didn't work, and her employee's paychecks were going to bounce. She asked for help from the taxpayer advocate, but they couldn't do anything. Worse, this was her busy season for her mistletoe sales (she was a mistletoe cultivator). If couldn't fill the orders, she didn't get income. Her life would be over, she feared.

Roberta wanted to know what we could do for her. Talking to her, I could tell she was a sophisticated, reasonable, organized person, which actually worried me. If someone as capable of her was unable to stop the IRS, then there must be some huge, hidden agenda going on.

I told her honestly, "We can't promise results, all I can promise is we will give it our best shot." I guess that was good enough because she hired us. She said quite confidently, "Something tells me you guys can do this."

Yet my stomach was turning, wondering if this was a case we should have taken.

Unfortunately, we were really up against it. Because of the failed previous attempts to get the levy off, we lost 14 days of our 20-day window to get the levy released and her money back. We had until the following Tuesday to get her money back, or it would be gone forever.

Vicky called the revenue officer, someone we'll refer to as "Ms. Charming." Ms. Charming was someone we'd never dealt with before at a field collection office. Vicki asked for her fax number so we could send her our power of attorney. Vicki said nothing else, but Ms. Charming added, "You know, that levy isn't coming off, so don't bother."

Well now. That sounded like a challenge.

We were still waiting for documents and transcripts on Wednesday. We closed the office for the holiday, and after a Thanksgiving dinner that couldn't be beat, we went back to work on Friday to see what could be done.

Remember, Roberta was a mistletoe farmer. And boy, the IRS just didn't seem to get the message for the holidays—employees' checks were going to bounce just in time for Christmas.

This is how the whole mess started. In 2001, Roberta owed payroll taxes on her farm employee wages of around $170,000. It was a cash-flow issue, and she was always behind. She always tried to pay the IRS something, but all that would happen is she would run up a new debt with them. She also went through a divorce and was massively distracted. She always thought she would sell her interest in the farm to pay back the IRS.

In fact, this is what she attempted to do on her own. Upon demand of Ms. Charming, unassisted, Roberta agreed to pay back the IRS $700 a month until she could sell her interest in the farm. By January 2011, she was supposed to have had the farm sold, but her asking price was way too optimistic—it needed to be high for her to have enough to pay of ff the IRS. She had no other assets, and because of the fact that mistletoe isn't as popular as it once was, she was in a struggling market and had problems making ends meet.

So in January, when the lump sum was due and she didn't have it, Roberta called the IRS Philadelphia payment center that was collecting her check. She told them there was no way she was going to pay off the lump sum, and she was wondering what she could do. The IRS told her not to worry and instructed her to continue making the $700 a month payments and that someone would be in touch with her to negotiate a new deal.

She heard nothing from the IRS until July, when she received a notice stating that the IRS didn't receive her installment amounts. She called and said she had proof of canceled checks. The IRS told her to send them, which she did.

In August, she got another threatening letter. The IRS said that if she didn't pay her installment agreement amounts, the IRS would levy her.

She called the number on this notice and explained to them that she had the copies of the canceled checks. She sent another letter to the person she spoke to proving that she wasn't in default of the agreement and continued making the monthly payments.

Then in September, she received a notice that said, "Thank you very much for your inquiry. Someone will be in touch with you in 30 days."

So now, dear readers, multiple-choice time. What would you guess happened next?

Here are your choices:

1. Someone at the IRS politely explained to Roberta that she was in actually in default of her installment agreement, not because she missed any of the $700 payments but rather because she never made the lump-sum payment that was due in January. And the people at the IRS who told her not to worry actually had no authority to extend her payoff date. It was all a terrible mix-up, and the IRS sees how Roberta could be so confused and are professionally and calmly able to enter into a new re-

payment schedule that's both feasible and realistic.

2. The case went back to revenue officer Charming, who without notice or even a courtesy phone call to Roberta, immediately levied and completely wipe out any business bank account Roberta happened to have, without once discussing all the correspondence Roberta had with the IRS about the defaulted agreement.

If you selected option two, you're a genius and your paranoia will serve you well for the rest of your life, because that's precisely what the IRS did.

To recap: The IRS told Roberta there was nothing to worry about, which was a complete and utter lie. After lying, the IRS completely wiped her out and devastated her, putting her in a horrible position, where her business—her sole, modest source of income—is about to be destroyed. Plus, she has to explain to her employees that she doesn't have the money to pay them. Not only are they going to be unemployed, but they won't even get the money she owes them!

This despite the fact that Roberta was detailed, responsible and reasonable with every communication with the IRS.

So now we were on a crusade. The U.S. Treasury has declared war on a hard-working American. We brought in our entire team on this one to figure out what could be done.

Again, Roberta already tried the taxpayer advocate and that failed miserably. Because of the sneakiness of this levy, we also lost other avenues to dispute. We figured our only course of action was to file an action under the Collection Appeal Program (CAP)—a rather a desperate ploy.

Very few CAPs are won by taxpayers for the simple reason that the standard of review of the IRS' actions are whether they broke the law or not. And to be honest, I didn't have all the facts, so I really didn't know what my basis would be exactly. But because it was Friday, and we had until Tuesday, I filed it anyway, hoping something would come up.

On Monday, Ms. Charming's acting supervisor, a group manager named "Vera," phoned me to discuss our CAP (they're required to attempt to settle the differences before the file is sent up). She was firm, nearly robotic in her explanation. Despite the fact that Roberta's employees will be irreparably harmed, she stated that the levy would remain in effect.

See, here's the thing. I talk to group managers all the time. Usually when they disagree with me, they have a pretty good reason that I have to address, and oftentimes, we can reach an agreement without the case going all the way to a CAP, which has a very unfavorable standard of review. This is why we prefer it when the client still has Collection Due Process (CDP) rights, which can be a much more favorable standard of review. Unfortunately for Roberta, those rights expired when she entered into the deal with Ms. Charming. So we were stuck with the CAP.

I was getting nowhere, so I did something I never had to do before. I requested the territory manager. Vera nearly leaped at volunteering her supervisor's contact info, which I didn't understand at the time but soon found out why.

I called the territory manager, "Ms. Grace." Ms. Grace immediately informed me that the decision to keep the levy was her call. And that there was no possible way the levy would be released.

I then understood why Vera so easily gave up Ms. Grace's contact info: Vera didn't think this levy was fair or a good idea, but she was under marching orders to not release the money.

I went over everything with Ms. Grace. I explained that releasing the funds and renegotiating the deal was actually in the best interest of the government. That if Roberta was able to continue operating her business she would be in a better position to pay back money to the IRS. Because if the IRS kept this money, this is all they would ever get—unless they were able to foreclosure on her half interest in a piece of farmland that was wouldn't even come close to paying half the debt. Our calculations were that Roberta had perhaps $60,000 she could get out of the property.

I was actually making some headway with Ms. Grace. She admitted that the original deal that Ms. Charming forced Roberta into was a stupid idea and wasn't realistic. "This is good," I thought to myself, "she's dumping on her own employee."

So I offered back, "Well, here's the thing, even if I get the levy released, we still have a problem that needs to be resolved. So why don't we work on a realistic solution that ends this forever."

Ms. Grace asked, "What do you have in mind."

"Offer in Compromise," I responded. "For 60K."

"That sounds wise, counselor." That's a nice compliment she gave me. "Let me look into some things, and I'll call you tomorrow to see if that's good."

I was pretty excited and pretty confident I was going to wrap up this case—in less than a week.

So the next day, which was the final Tuesday, our last possible day to get the money back, I anticipated a delightful conversation with Ms. Grace and the client.

But option two happened.

Ms. Grace told me, "No, I don't think that offer is good. We're keeping her money."

"Well, that's pretty shitty," I told her.

I hung up the phone and told the team, "No dice." We were going to have to win that CAP if we had any chance. Attorney Michelle Wynn was busy researching some law and the *Internal Revenue Manual*. Attorney Wynn—then my most recent hire from the Quinnipiac Law School legal clinic—was only an attorney for two months but was proving herself to be a tax wunderkind. She asked me for the copy of the August letter that Roberta got. "I have an idea," she said as I gave her the letter.

About two hours later, I heard an excited yell from her office "YES!"

I ran in, "What is it, Michelle?"

"Oh the IRS fucked this up good," a giddy Michelle was explaining. "The notice they sent in August only gives them the right to levy her state refunds checks. It doesn't allow them to levy bank accounts. And it says if you disagree, to contact them and the IRS will attempt to resolve it before taking any further action."

Michelle was nodding her head as I said, "And Roberta did contact them and attempt to resolve it."

At the same time, we both shouted, "WE HAVE PROOF!"

It was late at night, but I knew Ms. Grace was still working, so Michelle ran to the fax machine to send it to her while I was calling.

In a polite, yet forceful, tone I said, "Ms. Grace, I think your levy is illegal. Read my fax coming over."

"I'll call you back," she said.

Fifteen minutes later she called back.

"Half, Counselor. I'll give your back exactly half her money. And that is my final decision."

So we got half the money back, with about 15 minutes to spare! Not a bad result.

The other half, though, was gone for good, right?

Not quite—let's talk about option two.

Option two is where I told Ms. Grace, "Well, I sincerely appreciate that, but I can't stop at just half."

If a levy is illegal enough, it's actually possible to get the entire amount back after the 20-day deadline. I let Michelle do the CAP, as my emotions were getting the best of me. Plus, it was really her research that proved to be the winner, so I thought she should have the glory, if, in the rare, rare instance, she was able to get the entire levy released after the 20-day period.

On Thursday, a somewhat hostile appeals officer called. I was in the room on speakerphone. His tone was that he thought this appeal was a waste of his time and just vindictiveness on our part.

But Michelle calmly and precisely when over the documents and the law.

I could hear some surprise in his novice: "Let me call you back—I've got to do some research."

I went out for lunch, and we didn't hear back from the appeals officer.

The next day, I was working on a disclosure letter for another client. Vicki and Michelle stepped into my office. They stood in front of me.

They were smiling. I gave them that "what-the-hell-is-wrong-with-you" look.

"WE GOT EVERYTHING BACK!"

I fell out of my chair.

The appeals officer agreed with everything we said. We called Roberta to tell her. We could hear that she was crying. "I knew you guys would do this. I just knew it."

Now, I ask you, what would the IRS do next? Calmly renegotiate a deal with us, as clearly they've learned that we've got great chops and will fight for our clients until there's no fight left. Or be completely vindictive, so much so, that the U.S. government's position was harmed?

Yep, option two again. That's the popular choice, it appears.

To sum up the rest of the resolution, Roberta's case file is chock full of vindictive, petty actions by Ms. Charming—the revenue officer who took her marching orders from Ms. Grace.

Petty, unprofessional, illegal, incompetent and totally out of control—this is what the IRS can be.

Roberta is a sharp, careful woman. She really should have been able to negotiate a deal with the IRS on her own. But the fault isn't with Roberta. It's with the IRS. It's impossible to find enough qualified, intelligent, wise people to fill each desk. So they fill them with who they have.

If Roberta hired us when the problem first erupted, it would have remained small. The IRS never bothered to tell Roberta that if it comes down to making current tax payments or old payments, to always pay current. Second, we would have had our favorable CDP rights available so we could negotiate a realistic deal that would be the best option for both the U.S. Treasury and Roberta.

But Roberta, for as smart and organized as she was, was scared and just wanted the IRS to go away. So she agreed to something that was simply not realistic. And in a rush to close out a case, Ms. Charming forced a deal that wasn't going to happen. It was inevitable that Roberta wouldn't make her lump-sum payment.

If there's one lesson through all of this, it's this: Every big tax problem starts small. I really wish people would think about protecting themselves. Hiring a great tax attorney at this stage is something that must be addressed. Even if you're smart, organized, professional ad meticulously detailed, that's not enough. You need to know the law and how to work it.

Even though we ultimately prevailed, I wonder if the stress took years off of Roberta's life? And what about those employees during Christmas time? They were told they weren't going to be paid and would be laid off. What kind of stress did they go through?

What about morale at this IRS office? I'm sure Ms. Charming and Ms. Grace feel perfect and righteous about what they did, but their co-workers and subordinates must feel disgusted by such bullying and illegal actions.

You see, the truth is that most IRS revenue offices and managers are at least somewhat reasonable, so we're able to get resolutions faster and with less grief. My guess is that at the IRS holiday party, tens ton of mistletoe over Ms. Charming or Ms. Grace wouldn't even earn those two a wink.

About Anthony

Attorney Anthony E. Parent is a partner at Parent & Parent LLP and the founder of IRSmedic, a website dedicated to helping Americans find permanent tax relief from tough tax troubles.

While still in law school, Attorney Parent established himself as a prodigy by getting a criminal conviction overturned while still an intern. As he entered private practice, his appellate victories continued getting case after case overturned. However, once he discovered the desperate need for real tax relief, he applied his proven winning strategies to fighting the IRS.

He has developed a proven system to find the best resolution for every tax case and has been able to leverage his expertise to help thousands of taxpayers around the country and the globe. He's never shy about a tough challenge and is on the forefront of new IRS offshore initiatives. Attorney Parent serves as source of inspiration for his staff and clients by instilling a resolute faith that the best solution may be just one sentence away.

CHAPTER 9

Protecting Consumers From Large Corporations

By Ken Hardison

Oftentimes the term "ambulance chaser" is used to describe injury lawyers, a set of lawyers who work very hard to ensure individuals' rights are upheld after becoming a victim of negligence or injury due to another person's carelessness. The tireless efforts of injury lawyers are often overlooked, and they're vilified in the media. Let's be honest: People believe personal injury lawyers file frivolous lawsuits for ridiculously high amounts of money.

Lawyers actually protect and defend consumers from America's large corporations. Below are the actual facts from the McDonald's hot coffee case, an excellent example of how lawyers protect consumers on a daily basis.

In 1992, a 79-year-old woman, Stella Liebeck, sat in the passenger seat of the car as her grandson drove through the McDonald's drive-thru and ordered her a 49 cent cup of coffee. After she received her beverage, her grandson pulled into a parking spot so she could add cream and sugar. She placed the cup of coffee between her knees to pry off the lid. When she attempted to pull off the lid, the entire cup of coffee spilled onto her thighs, buttocks and groin. To make matters worse, she was wearing cotton sweatpants, which absorbed the liquid, causing it to stay against her skin. She received third-degree burns on 6 percent of her body and lesser burns over 16 percent. Spending eight days in the hospital undergoing skin graft surgeries, she lost 20 percent of her body weight and endured two more years of continued medical treatment after her release.

Liebeck wrote to McDonald's requesting a settlement of $20,000 to cover her medical bills, which were around $11,000, the remainder of which was to be for her daughter's lost wages during the time she was taking care of her mother. McDonald's refused this offer, instead offering her $800. She soon hired a lawyer and sued McDonald's for "gross negligence" (or serious carelessness) for selling coffee that was "unreasonably dangerous" and "defectively manufactured." Liebeck tried to settle the case out of court twice, offering to settle for $90,000 and then offering a settlement of $225,000 at the suggestion of a mediator, yet McDonald's flatly refused all offers to settle. So off to court they went!

Some interesting facts arose during the seven-day trial, including that *McDonald's had received more than 700 reports of injuries due to the extra hot coffee.* McDonald's coffee was kept at a steamy 180-190 degrees. At this temperature it takes approximately two to seven seconds for third-degree burns to occur. If the temperature was reduced a mere 20 degrees, to a temperature of 160 degrees, it would take more than 20 seconds for serious burns, which would still require skin grafting. This extra time, although it may not seem like much, would have given Liebeck time to remove the hot liquid from her skin or at least attempt to do so.

McDonald's claimed that the reason for serving such hot coffee was that those who purchased the coffee were typically commuters who wanted to drive a distance with the coffee and then consume it once they reached their destinations, so the high initial temperature was meant to keep the coffee hot during customers' commutes. However, this contradicts the company's own research that showed customers intended to consume the coffee while driving *to* their destinations. These facts, including the hot coffee temperatures and previous complaints, to which McDonald's executives testified to previous knowledge of, along with their defense being in contradiction with their own research, are a few details that are believed to have lead to such a large punitive settlement. Some jurors made comments about "wanting to teach McDonald's a lesson" and show them that ignoring customer complaints and taking advantage of them is unacceptable behavior and won't be tolerated.

Armed with this knowledge, a 12-member jury applied the principles of "comparative negligence," meaning that they felt both parties were at fault, but one more so than the other. They ruled McDonald's to be 80 percent at fault for Liebeck's injuries, and Liebeck was found to be 20 percent at fault. The jury decided she should receive compensatory damages (money to cover the cost of her injuries) in the amount of $160,000. They also awarded her punitive damages (a fine that the defendant has to pay) to the amount of $2.7 million, the amount equivalent to two days worth of McDonald's coffee sales, to penalize McDonald's for their negligent actions. However, the judge reduced punitive damages to $480,000, which was still three times the compensatory amount awarded, for a total settlement of $640,000.

Both McDonald's and Liebeck appealed the decision in December 1994, but the parties decided to settle out of court for an undisclosed amount rumored to be less than $600,000. Unfortunately, we'll never know exactly what the amount of the settlement was for the infamous case, since Liebeck signed a secrecy order as part of her financial settlement. This is another reason the media didn't accurately represent the details of this case as neither McDonald's nor Liebeck were ever able to disclose any information regarding the case or the settlement they finally reached.

Lawyers protect those who can't protect themselves. The McDonalds case is a clear example of how one woman with the aid of an excellent lawyer held McDonald's accountable for it's failure to protect their customers for the sake of profits over people's safety.

About Ken

Growing up in Dunn, North Carolina, Ken Hardison decided he wanted to become an attorney after seeing many of the hard-working families and individuals in the Dunn area being taken advantage of by those who knew how to apply the law. He wanted to be the one that leveled the playing field.

After completing his undergraduate work at Campbell University, where he graduated with honors, Ken enrolled in Norman Adrian Wiggins School of Law at Campbell University. Upon receiving his Juris Doctorate in 1982, he quickly went into practice in Dunn, North Carolina.

In 27 years of practice, Ken has acquired many accolades, which he attributes to his focused attention to each and every client he represents. From being voted one of the Top 100 Trial Lawyers in North Carolina to being a member of the Million Dollar Advocates Forum, it's easy to see he's passionate about his clients and serious about the quality of their representation.

Ken's ethics, integrity and standards have set the path for which the firm operates on a daily basis. He's described by attorneys and staff as someone who puts the client first, is very experienced, and is always willing to help no matter the problem.

CHAPTER 10

29 Insurance Adjuster Tactics That Can Cost You

By Ken Nunn

When you're involved in an accident or suffer a personal injury, you need the right fighter on your side. As an injury attorney who has stood up for the rights of accident victims in Indiana communities for more than 44 years, I've always worked hard to make sure my clients get the justice they deserve.

If you've been hurt due to another's negligence, you could be facing overwhelming medical bills as well as lost wages, and, in some cases, a lifetime of pain and suffering. Sometimes families are even forced to suffer the loss of a loved one. That's why my law firm goes after every dollar my clients deserve—and I mean *every* dollar.

Unfortunately, some people don't think they need a lawyer such as myself to fight for their rights. In most cases, they're offered much, much less than they're entitled to by the insurance company involved in their case—and accept it because they think that's all they can get.

That's what the insurance companies want you to believe. In this chapter, I'd like to showcase 29 tactics that insurance adjusters use to rob you of your rights and push you into settling for less than you should. Beware of these tactics, because, if they're successful, they can cost you plenty of money!

Tactic #1: Adjuster does* not *call you within a week of your accident: If you do *not* hear from an adjuster within one week of the accident, it could mean that the company is understaffed, ignoring your claim, or that the other party wasn't insured after all.

Tactic #2: Adjuster does* not *want to put anything in writing: Insist that the adjuster provide you with a letter identifying himself and his company. That letter should indicate the policy and claim numbers, and, most important, it should confirm that the company provided coverage for the negligent party on the date of the accident.

Tactic #3: Adjuster refuses to tell you the policy limits: You should request that the adjuster disclose the negligent party's policy limits in writing. If the adjuster refuses, that's definitely a cue to contact a lawyer such as myself to handle your case. If you're seriously injured, you need to know the limits.

Tactic #4: Adjuster refuses to confirm that the wrong-doer was at fault: Ask the adjuster to provide you with a letter stating that the person his or her company insures was at fault and caused the accident. If the adjuster does *not* believe that their insured was completely at fault, request that the adjuster explain, in writing, why you or someone else is partially at fault.

Tactic #5: Adjuster wants to tape record or video you: Don't let anyone record you, especially if an attorney isn't present. If you accidentally give incorrect answers, it could cost you a lot of money, or even your whole case. Before you give a statement, you should talk to a lawyer first. Remember, a recorded statement can be used as *evidence against you.*

Tactic #6: Adjuster wants you to sign a written medical release: Most insurance companies want you to sign a "general wide-open release" for your medical records, but it's more information than they're entitled to. *Check with a lawyer before signing anything—don't sign away any rights!*

Tactic #7: The insurance company wants "their doctor" to examine you: If the insurance adjuster tells you there will be no settlement unless you're examined by "their doctor," you need to talk to a lawyer first because you may be walking into a trap. An experienced injury lawyer can tell you all the rights you have pertaining to your case.

Tactic #8: Adjuster refuses to put settlement offers in writing: Ask the adjuster to put all settlement offers on your case in writing. If he refuses, you should be concerned. Verbal settlement offers are sometimes forgotten by the adjuster.

Tactic #9: Adjuster is dodging you: If it's difficult for you to contact the adjuster or he seems to be putting you off, he may be using "a delay tactic" on your case. Delays can cost you money, which is why so many of these tactics are designed to make you wait for little or no reason.

Tactic #10: Surprise, unannounced visits from the adjuster: If the insurance adjuster shows up *without* an appointment at your home...again, *you should be concerned.* The purpose of such a visit may be to catch you doing something that hurts your case or to demonstrate that you're *not* injured. Refuse to discuss your case and tell the adjuster to call back for an appointment.

Tactic #11: Insurance company conducts surveillance of you: If the adjuster or the insurance company investigator is asking your neighbors, employer, co-workers, friends or doctors questions about you without your permission—or even conducting video surveillance on you—make sure you get in touch with a lawyer ASAP!

Tactic #12: Adjuster offers you a tiny check: If the adjuster refuses to pay you anything for your claim or offers to pay you a small amount, you need a lawyer. Just because the adjuster tells you your case is worth a small amount, doesn't necessarily mean he's right. Ask the adjuster to put his reasons for such an offer in writing.

Tactic #13: Adjuster says you don't need a lawyer: If the adjuster says you don't need a lawyer, or he tells you *not* to obtain legal advice, you would be justified in being concerned about why the insurance company is so anxious to keep you away from a lawyer. Could it be that the adjuster doesn't want you to know the true value of your case or wants to keep you in the dark about your legal rights? A consultation with an injury lawyer such as myself is usually free—and definitely worth your time!

Tactic #14: Adjuster delays by using an answering machine or voicemail: Sometimes adjusters avoid your calls and rely on voicemails and other message systems that allow them to delay the settlement of your case.

Tactic #15: Adjuster keeps asking for more medical records. The insurance company claims it needs more and more medical reports, so you provide those records. Then the insurance company requests more and *more* records. This is a common delaying tactic used by insurance companies. The insurance company also may demand copies of your income tax returns for the past five years or some other private information about you. Again, a lawyer will tell you what your rights are in this situation.

Tactic #16: Adjuster says he's seeking more "dollar authority": The insurance adjustor may say he needs permission to offer a higher settlement figure and needs that "dollar authority" from a supervisor. Sometimes that bureaucratic process can take weeks or even months. The adjuster is hoping you do *not* want to wait, so you'll take a smaller settlement *now*. Also, you should know that adjusters *hate* asking for more dollar authority. Their bosses will *not* be happy. The adjuster is expected to settle the case for the original dollar authority, which can be very low.

Tactic #17: Adjuster is on a two-week vacation: You're told the adjuster is out for a few weeks, and there's no one else to talk to. Insurance companies love this delay tactic. Most other types of businesses would have a designated substitute to help out, but not insurance companies that want to delay your settlement.

Tactic #18: Adjuster has been transferred to other cases: You're told the adjuster you were dealing with has been transferred to other cases, and it will take two, three or more weeks for the new adjuster to become familiar with yours. It's common for insurance companies to reassign adjusters, and, for each reassignment, there's a built-in delay.

Tactic #19: Your case gets transferred: As another delaying tactic, you're told your file has gone back to the home office for review and won't be back for several weeks or months.

Tactic #20: Your adjuster is on "weather assignment": You're notified the adjuster has been temporarily reassigned due to hurricane, earthquake or storm damage. The adjuster will talk to you about your case when he returns. Usually no other adjuster will step forward to help you settle your case, so, again, *you're forced to wait.*

Tactic #21: There's been a permanent change of adjuster: Some adjusters simply quit or they're fired. Another guaranteed delay, because *you* have to wait for a new adjuster to be assigned to your case.

Tactic #22: They're too nice to you: Ordinarily, you might not see this as a problem, but it very well might be. The adjuster may have been trained to be nice so you believe you'll receive the amount you're entitled to. That way, you won't hire a lawyer because you want to "wait and see" what the insurance company offers. The insurance company likes this, because it's like holding a carrot on a stick out in front of you and watching you run after it. Meanwhile, every day of delay helps the insurance company receive more interest on the money they legally owe you. Also, if they stall you long enough and you get far enough behind in your bills, then you'll be more likely to take a tiny check out of desperation. I've focused so much on their delay tactics because it's the insurance company's biggest weapon against you. When you decide to just "wait and see," you actually help the insurance adjuster gradually weaken you—financially, physically and mentally—until you cave in and take a small settlement.

Tactic #23: Adjuster makes you feel guilty: The adjuster explains to you that if everybody accepts smaller settlements, insurance rates will be lower for the general public and the savings will be passed on to all policyholders (because, as you all know, companies aren't interested in keeping that money—yeah, right). Or maybe the adjuster wants you to feel sorry for the insured party that's responsible for your injury and not go after what you're entitled to. Never, never feel guilty about being compensated for your pain and suffering, lost wages and medical bills. A tiny check—or *no* check—just means the CEO or president of the insurance company gets a bigger salary and a bigger bonus.

Tactic #24: "Hiding the Ball": In this tactic, the insurance adjuster will *not* volunteer anything to help you realize and understand how your own insurance coverage plays a part in your settlement. You may have thousands of dollars coming to you from your underinsurance coverage. It is *not* the adjuster's job to help you with underinsurance. For example, in Indiana, there are little-known laws relating to this situation that can help you. Injured people have lost thousands upon thousands of dollars because they do *not* fully understand their legal rights....and they don't even know that they've just lost $25,000 to $75,000 *(or even more)!*

Tactic #25: The "Bogus Claims Committee": The adjuster tells you that your claim must first go before a "committee." The adjuster may be buying time and stalling, so don't be surprised if there's no committee, or if the so-called committee is made up of the adjuster himself....and no one else!

Tactic #26: Insurance company delays...hoping you'll die: This isn't pleasant to think about, but it's a possibility. If you're elderly, the insurance adjuster might decide to stall instead of processing your claim, hoping you may die before they have to pay you. Never forget that the insurance business is a heartless one. They're only interested in *money and profits*—and you'd be very surprised by how many times this tactic is actually used by insurance companies.

Tactic #27: No one controls what the adjuster says: Many insurance adjusters operate out of their homes. They're *not* part of the home office or in some high-rise building where their conversations can be overheard by their fellow employees. When they talk to you on the phone, they can say anything they want and no supervisor will hear the conversation. As a result, these adjusters will say and argue *anything* to pressure you into taking a very tiny check.

Tactic #28: The rental car gets called in: If your car can't be repaired as a result of the accident, your car will be considered "totaled." A common tactic for the insurance company is to put you into a rental car immediately, then, several days later, they'll make you a very low settlement offer for your car and put pressure on you. At the same time they make their settlement offer, they might demand that you return the rental car within the next 48 hours.

A lot of people have no choice but to say yes to the small settlement amount. Many times, the car is worth a lot more than what's being offered. The insurance companies can save millions and millions of dollars by using this tactic.

Tactic #29: Rigged computers: Rigged computers have literally *saved* millions of dollars for the insurance companies. Here's how they work: The insurance company programs a computer to their specifications, then inputs information about cases. The computer then spits out a ridiculously low settlement offer, and, unfortunately, a lot of people say yes to that offer.

This works because the insurance companies know that a certain percentage of the people will say yes, even to a tiny check. The insurance company has a clear advantage—more money, lawyers, knowledge and experience—and it has *not* suffered the injuries and worries you have. The adjuster is under no pressure at all, whereas you and your family are under tremendous pressure.

In general, the 29 tactics I've detailed in this chapter are designed to take advantage of victims without legal representation, coercing them into signing away important rights, giving away valuable information, and growing so stressed about the situation that they're likely to accept a settlement that can be tens of thousands of dollars less than they are entitled to.

Dealing with an insurance adjuster can be like going down a one-way street: The adjuster wants you to accommodate his every request while he works on a way for the insurance company to give you nothing—or as little as possible.

Don't accept endless delays or less than you should receive. Consult with an experienced injury lawyer such as myself and find out what your rights are. You have nothing to lose....unless you believe everything the insurance company tells you!

About Ken

Ken Nunn is the sole owner of the Ken Nunn Law Office in Bloomington, Indiana, which limits its practice exclusively to personal injury and wrongful death cases. For more than 44 years, the firm has built a strong reputation as a defender of victims' rights, having represented more than 23,000 injury and wrongful death clients over the past four and a half decades. The law offices consist of 11 attorneys and approximately 65 support staff members, as well as six retired state troopers who serve as investigators for the firm.

The Ken Nunn Law Office has been ranked No. 1 by the *Jury Verdict Reporter* for the past nine years for doing the most jury trials in Indiana for injured plaintiffs; Ken himself has completed more than 40 trials as first chair. In 2009, the firm obtained a $157 million judgment for a wrongful death case, the largest jury verdict in the history of Indiana and the ninth largest nationally that year, and also obtained the largest jury verdict in Monroe County, Indiana, $15 million, on behalf of an injured child.

Ken received his Bachelor of Science degree in business in 1964 from the Indiana University School of Business, and he received his Juris Doctor degree in 1967 from the Indiana University School of Law. At that time, he was admitted to practice law in all state and federal courts in Indiana.

Ken is a member of the Million Dollar Advocates Forum and the Multi-Million Dollar Advocates Forum, and is listed in the *Top Trial Lawyers in America.* He has been listed as an Indiana Super Lawyer and is a member of the American Association for Justice, the Indiana State Bar Association, and the Indiana Trial Lawyers Association. He's on the National Advisory Board of APITLA (Association of Plaintiff Interstate Trucking Lawyers of America) and has been a guest lecturer at Indiana University, both to undergraduates as well as students at the IU School of Law.

Married for 49 years, Ken and his wife, Leah, have two children, Vicky and David, and two grandchildren. Vicky serves as a litigation attorney in the Ken Nunn Law Office. Ken was listed in the 2012 edition of *Who's Who of America,* and was also commissioned a Kentucky Colonel by the governor of Kentucky.

CHAPTER 11

Trucking Accidents: The Growing Danger on Our Roads

By Michael D. Ponce

It was January 25, 2006, on an ordinary Wednesday afternoon, and Alvin Wilkerson was exhausted. He had good reason to be; he'd been driving his truck for more than 34 hours straight. His tractor-trailer was loaded with a delivery of bottled water and weighed in at almost 80,000 pounds.

He was entering the small town of Lake Butler, Florida, just as the local schools were wrapping up their day. School zone lights were flashing and the stop sign of the yellow school bus in front of him was out and plainly visible. Unfortunately, Wilkerson was too tired to notice—and a few tragic moments later, seven school children would lose their lives and nine others would be seriously injured in the fiery crash that ensued.

Each week, more than a hundred American citizens are killed in crashes involving large commercial trucks, according to an Associated Press story from March 12, 2007. That adds up to a tragic toll of more than 5,000 people a year across the country, not to mention the 114,000 Americans who are seriously injured every year in such accidents.

Unfortunately, both the trucking industry and the federal government aren't doing enough to prevent this nightmarish scenario from recurring. As a personal injury attorney in Nashville, I routinely represent clients who are involved in these kinds of horrible events. In this chapter, I'd like to discuss the reasons behind the alarmingly high number of tragic trucking accidents and how to protect yourself legally should you find yourself involved in one.

WHY TRUCK ACCIDENTS HAPPEN

One of the main causes of these types of accidents is what played a part in Alvin Wilkerson's crash: driver exhaustion. And yet, despite the large number of fatalities involved, the Federal Motor Carrier Safety Administration, the agency that Congress created in 1999 to promote public safety on the highways, has actually *increased* the number of hours a driver can operate a truck by *28 percent* since 2003, relaxing requirements that had been in place since the 1930s.

That could mean a truck driver is behind the wheel as many as 88 hours a week—and even that legal limit is often ignored. Generally, trucking companies pay drivers based on the number of miles they drive, rather than a per hour rate. That means the main incentive for truck drivers is to drive as fast as possible for as long as possible, creating an incredible potential for dangerous accidents that are tragic both for the victims as well as the truck drivers.

Another legal requirement that's supposed to make the trucking industry safer is that drivers must maintain log books so that law enforcement agencies, as well as the trucking companies, can monitor driver activity to ensure compliance with regulations. Unfortunately, trucking companies all too often fail to check those log books for safety violations, and, of course, those log books can easily be filled with false information by drivers determined to earn as much as they can.

That can lead to catastrophic results. For example, a recent client of mine was traveling on Interstate 40 in Tennessee when a tractor-trailer suddenly veered into her lane. In order to avoid a crash, she moved her car as far to the left as possible, putting her on the shoulder of the road next to a concrete divider. But the fatigued truck driver continued to drift further toward her, pinning her car between the eighteen-wheeler and the divider, and trapping it between the two as it continued down the road.

When law enforcement officials arrived at the accident scene, they inspected the truck. What they found was not one log book, but *two* separate ones covering the same time period. One log book had a written record of what actually was going on, and the other was designed to provide the "official" false record that demonstrated legal compliance.

Why has the government not done more to address this deadly problem? According to public interest groups such as Citizens for Reliable and Safe Highways (CRASH), it's because the Federal Motor Carrier Safety Administration has been co-opted by the trucking industry. Those groups believe that the agency's regulators are more concerned with future employment opportunities with the truck companies than with creating new rules that might increase safety but decrease profits.

STEPS NEED TO BE TAKEN

The sad fact is there are many relatively easy and inexpensive steps that could be taken to reduce the number of trucking accidents. First and foremost is to *reverse the trend of deregulation in the trucking industry*. Allowable hours of driving time need to be decreased, and, to further ensure compliance beyond the outdated practice of driver-completed log books, *GPS-enabled onboard electronic records* should be required. These records should monitor hours of service. In this age of sophisticated electronic surveillance, this should be a no-brainer, yet the trucking industry continues to successfully lobby against the implementation of this technology.

Another simple fix would be to require trucks to have *tamperproof governors in place* to limit just how fast the truck could go. This would prevent any dangerous speeding that could lead to an 80,000-pound truck going out of control.

Finally, *a shift to shipping more cargo by rail* rather than by trucking would also significantly reduce the number of highway deaths. Other side benefits would include eliminating congestion from our nation's roadways as well as making a lower carbon footprint on the environment.

These types of simple modifications to regulations and attitudes, in combination with providing better training to truck drivers, would undoubtedly save thousands of lives each year. Until safety on the roads is improved, however, it's vitally important that citizens stand up to the trucking industry and hold them responsible for the high number of tragic accidents. Responsible companies and safe drivers should definitely be rewarded, but, at the same time, trucking companies that put unsafe vehicles on the road or provide pay incentives to drivers who buck already-inadequate safety regulations must be held accountable.

Instead, these trucking companies have rapid-response teams of lawyers and investigators in place so when a serious crash occurs; they're immediately deployed to the scene in an attempt to further block legal repercussions. That's because they know these huge vehicles hurtling at high speeds on the interstate highways can cause tremendous damage and they want to avoid as much liability as possible.

Jacqueline Gillan, vice president of Advocates for Highway and Auto Safety, says, "Anytime there is an E. coli outbreak, the federal government uses every resource available to stop this public health threat. Yet unsafe big rigs kill and maim tens of thousands each year because truckers are pushed to drive long hours under unsafe operating conditions while the federal response has been silence and indifference."

Again, 5,000 Americans die each year in trucking accidents. The average yearly toll from E. coli? 61.

IF YOU'RE INVOLVED IN A TRUCKING ACCIDENT

When you're involved in any kind of crash, you're bound to feel overwhelmed and stressed, especially if you or another person has been seriously injured and there has been a great deal of physical damage. A truck accident, because of the weight and size of the vehicle, has the potential to be worse than those just involving normal cars—and cause you even more emotional strain.

Nonetheless, you should always do everything you can to protect yourself legally (and physically) in the immediate aftermath of the accident. These important steps include:

1. *Call 911.* Then request all necessary emergency service personnel.

2. *Get medical attention.* Even when accident victims aren't at fault, they often feel reluctant and even embarrassed to accept immediate medical attention. The rush of adrenaline that

can flood a person's body following the trauma of a crash can make it difficult for that person to accurately assess the extent of any injuries. That's why seeking medical care should be a priority.

3. *Preserve evidence from the accident scene.* Most large trucks are equipped with an "accident kit," which is *not* a first aid kit but rather a set of instructions that drivers are supposed to follow to provide evidence. Typically, this kit contains a camera to take photos of the scene and vehicles involved, forms to obtain the contact information of any bystanders/witnesses, and forms to diagram the crash. As noted, some trucking companies have special legal teams that will be deployed to the accident scene ASAP. Individuals, however, most likely don't have those kinds of resources; you can, however, request that law enforcement officers who are present take pictures of the scene, or you or any other person who's physically able can take photos as well.

4. *Contact an experienced trucking litigation firm.* While obviously your health and safety (as well as the medical condition of any other injured party) must be your primary concern, you should get legal help as soon as possible. A firm that specializes in trucking litigation should be able to "even the score" when it comes to going up against their corporate resources. Some of these types of firms even have their own rapid-response teams that will come to the scene of an accident and ensure the preservation of critical evidence on the victim's behalf.

WHY QUICK LEGAL HELP IS VITAL TO YOUR CASE

The reason both trucking companies and trucking litigation law firms want to get to the scene of the crash so quickly is because the longer the delay in investigating the accident, the more the evidence can be compromised. Tire marks often fade quickly, fluid spills can be washed away with the next rain, and, as time passes, it may become difficult to link any road markings to the crash in question.

A well-trained investigator will:

- Examine tire marks, gouges, scrapes, fluid spills, glass, and any other debris or markings on the road.
- Locate and record the final resting point of all vehicles.
- Document the road surface conditions; smooth, cracked rough, or potholed.
- Place an inclinometer on the road to show the grade of any incline and photograph the inclinometer readings.
- Videotape the approach to the point of impact from each driver's perspective.
- Note the site distances given the heights of the vehicles.
- Document with diagrams that are supported by photographs and measurements.
- Inspect the vehicles involved. This includes photographing and documenting all property damage and taking photos of the tires to show their condition, as well as recording the weight, height and VIN number for each vehicle. Vehicle lights will also be examined to see if they're in working order.
- Attempt to get access to the truck driver's log book and photograph each page of the log book in order.

Experienced trucking litigators are also aware that tractor-trailers are frequently equipped with other helpful tools to gather evidence and information. For example, all tractor-trailer engines built after 1992 have ECMs (engine control modules) in place. These are engine-mounted computers whose original purpose was to increase engine efficiency by monitoring its ongoing usage.

A legal investigator can download data that the EMC collects, which could be helpful to your case. That data includes the speeds at which the engine was running, as well as the number of hours it has spent running, idling and turned off. The EMCs in newer tractor-trailer engines also record hard stops. All of this vital data must be downloaded quickly, because, when the truck is put back into operation, the relevant EMC data can be overwritten with newer information.

SELECTING THE RIGHT LAWYER

If you're in a need of legal representation in a trucking crash (or any other type of crash, for that matter), there are a few questions you should ask a prospective attorney.

1. *Does the attorney specialize in the area of law that pertains to your case?* Just like doctors, attorneys specialize in different areas. You obviously want a lawyer who knows the intricacies and complexities involved in your specific case.

2. *How many years has the attorney been practicing?* Experience counts. You want a lawyer who knows what he or she is doing and has successfully dealt with a number of similar cases.

3. *Does your attorney have the financial resources to prosecute an expensive trucking litigation?* A good legal firm will be able to make the right investment in your case if they think you have a legitimate case. That investment includes a full investigation of the crash in question by their hand-picked team of experts.

4. *Is the attorney in good standing by the bar?* If they're not, you might want to steer clear. You want someone who doesn't have any professional baggage that would weigh you down.

5. *What do the attorney's past clients say about him or her?* To fully answer this question, you may need to do some research on your own. Look for reliable and objective online reviews, comments or news stories by Googling the name of the attorney and/ or the legal firm.

6. *What awards and distinctions does the attorney have?* This is something else you may be able to uncover online, or you can simply ask the attorney in question.

7. *Does the attorney speak to professional legal organizations?* If they do, it will indicate a high standing among peers as well as a high level of expertise.

8. *Is the attorney certified as a civil trial specialist?* This can be critical to your case. Many attorneys take the easy way out and settle virtually all their cases. This means they often don't obtain the best possible results for their clients. That's because the insurance companies know they won't have to be challenged in court and can get away with offering lower settlements. Your

attorney should have a good trial track record, because even if your case doesn't go to court, the opposition will know it very possibly could and, as a result, will usually offer a better settlement amount.

All of us at our legal firm, Michael D. Ponce & Associates, work hard to provide the best possible service to our clients. If you or someone you know has the misfortune to be involved in a trucking accident, please feel free to contact us through our website at www.poncelaw.com for more information about how to handle your case.

About Michael

Managing Attorney and Senior Litigator

Michael D. Ponce is certified as a Civil Trial Specialist by the Tennessee Commission on Continuing Legal Education, and Board Certified as a Civil Trial Advocate by the National Board of Trial Advocacy. He's also a member of the American Bar Association, the Nashville Bar Association, Tennessee Trial Lawyers Association, American Association for Justice.

Mr. Ponce is a former clerk to Hon. Judge John Wisdom, U.S. Court of Appeals (5th Cir.). He received his Juris Doctor cum laude from Tulane University in New Orleans. He also has an MBA and a BS from Suffolk University in Boston.

Noteworthy Appellate Cases

Montgomery v Wal-Mart Stores, Inc.,
No. M2001-01718-WC-R3-CV, 2002
2002 WL 1364028
(Tenn. W.C. Panel 2002)

Seminars Taught

Damages in Tennessee Civil Trial Practice, NBI

Balancing Ethics and Professionalism in the
Law for Tennessee Attorneys, NBI

Auto Accident & Evidence Reconstruction, NBI

Awards and Recognitions

Million Dollar Advocates

Super Lawyers

CHAPTER 12

Don't Get Hit Twice: Avoid Repaying Health Insurance Expenses After an Accident

By Mark C. Blane, Esq.

If you or a family member sustain injuries from an accident, and all or part of your medical care is covered under a private health insurance plan, did you know you'll have to pay back the health plan what it paid out in medical services if you end up with a settlement from the at-fault party?

Yes, it's true! All 50 states have their own individual law on this, but as a general rule, you can expect to face your own private health insurance in a negotiation for reimbursement when you settle your personal injury case, provided they paid out some or all of your medical care from an accident due to a negligent person or entity. That's why your health insurance is like a "glorified loan" when it comes to personal injury settlements.

You may ask yourself, why is this legal when you pay monthly premiums to your, or your family's, health plan? It seems like you're paying twice, right? One time on the monthly premiums and another time when you get a settlement from an injury due to someone else's negligence.

State law allows health insurance companies the legal right to collect (subrogate) what they paid out for medical care on your injury settlement from a wrong-doer because your injury settlement will normally contain the following two items:

1. *Special Damages:* These are funds for any wage loss, out-of-pocket expenses, and your reasonable and necessary medical bills (that were covered under your health plan). They're known as "special damages," since they're for precise and documentable items such as medical bills and the like.

2. *General Damages:* These are funds for what's known as pain and suffering damages. They're known as "general damages," since they're harder to calculate, i.e., a particular injury could affect various people differently, depending on their injuries and medical care endured.

The focus of this issue lies in number 2 (General Damages) because the states assume you'll be getting a good settlement for general damages (pain and suffering) in connection with your special damages (medical bills, wage loss, etc.). Therefore, the logic is the health insurance company is entitled to get paid back what it paid out because you're going to get a good or adequate recovery. But the logic is flawed to the extent that not everyone gets a good, fair or adequate settlement. For example, what happens if you get a settlement from a person that only has minimal insurance coverage? Is it your fault that you now have to argue with your own health insurance on their reimbursement rights? Well, it's not all doom and gloom because this chapter is designed to show you what you can do about it!

HIRE A GOOD INJURY LAWYER

The first thing you can do to combat your health insurance reimbursement negotiation is to locate and retain a good injury lawyer to settle your case. You're probably asking yourself, why do that because he or she will charge me attorneys' fees on top of what I have to pay back my private health plan? While that may be true, a good injury lawyer has legal weapons (arguments) in his or her arsenal to help combat the health plan being paid back *any amount* from your settlement. He or she has the legal knowledge and experience to navigate the stormy waters of health insurance subrogation law when you more than likely have no or little experience to navigate! A good injury lawyer must be a good negotiator, not only to obtain the case value from the at-fault party on the front-end but equally be a skilled negotiator with your own health insurance company on the back-end.

For example, most states recognize powerful legal doctrines known as the *make whole doctrine* and the *common fund doctrine*. The make whole doctrine basically says that a health insurance company has to first make sure that a person is *made whole*, or receives a fair compensation in net recovery from a settlement, before it can assert its health reimbursement rights, known as "subrogation rights."

A lawyer can help argue what's fair and what's not. Many factors are taken into consideration, ranging from whether you had any lost wages that were not, for any reason, properly accounted for in the settlement with the at-fault party's insurance to whether part or all of your settlement truly comes directly from the at-fault party. For example, you may have an exclusion in your private health insurance plan that doesn't allow for reimbursement if you trigger your uninsured motorist benefits to compensate you or your family member for injuries due to a person who had no insurance. You may even have inadequate language in your health insurance plan that a lawyer can find to argue no reimbursement whatsoever! Remember, if your state recognizes the make whole doctrine, then they have to first take into consideration these and many more factors to see what amount is fair for reimbursement.

If your state allows the *common fund doctrine,* then your injury lawyer can offset his or her fees and costs in obtaining your settlement against what has to be paid back to your health plan. This means the lawyer can reduce between 33 to 40 percent (depending if your lawyer had to fight for the settlement after filing a lawsuit) of what your health plan is demanding back as payment from your settlement. The logic here is it isn't fair for a health insurance company to "piggyback ride" on your private choice to hire an injury lawyer and pay him or her a contingency fee to get your settlement only to then pay back, dollar-for-dollar, your private health plan when they risked nothing in terms of attorney's fees and costs. Thus, under the common fund doctrine, a good injury lawyer will use this to reduce what you have to pay back your health insurance. This savings can many times usurp the costs of hiring an injury lawyer in the first place.

REVIEW YOUR PRIVATE HEALTH PLAN

If you own your own business or work for somebody else, you have the right as a beneficiary of your health plan to review what it's subrogation policy is when you get injured by somebody else (also known as a third party). This is important because your own health plan is required to have in writing its policies, procedures and limits of what it can and cannot do in these circumstances.

What you need to do is review your Summary Plan Description (known as the "SPD") that comes with your health insurance policy. You should have a copy, but if you don't, ask your employer's human resources department to provide you with one. The SPD is the primary source of information for workers who participate in an employment-based health care plan. When you get your SPD, look up in the table of contents any language referencing "reimbursement" or "subrogation clauses." See what it says about reimbursement to the health plan when you get injured by someone else and what limits it may or may not have. Also, if you have health insurance tied to your automobile policy, which is known in some states as either "medical pay benefits (med pay)," or "personal injury protection (PIP protection)," check out whether or not you have an exclusions to pay them back anything. Believe it or not, some of these policies contain non-reimbursement clauses.

The point here is you should be aware of your health insurance coverage—in all of its various forms—and what will happen if you get injured by someone else and get medical care that leads to a settlement. Preparation is key, and sometimes that requires a little reading and study, but this way there will be no surprises later.

HOW YOU OBTAIN A SETTLEMENT
MAY MAKE A DIFFERENCE

Depending on *how* you obtain a settlement in an injury case may make a huge difference on what your health plan can legally collect, if they can at all! For example, say you're injured in a car accident, but the at-fault party had no insurance, so you had to file a claim under your own car insurance for uninsured motorist benefits. All your medical care was covered by your private health plan. It could be that your private health plan has an exclusion to collect any money if the majority of your settlement came from "first party funds." First party funds is insurance money from a policy that protected you, not the at-fault third party, which is known as "third party" funds. The reason why these exclusions exist is because it's not fair to punish you further after you were injured by a negligent party, and you were responsible enough to have first party coverage (like uninsured motorist) in place, which you're paying monthly premiums for, only to be hounded by your health insurance for more money from that settlement!

How do you know if your plan has this type of exclusion? Check your SPD. Also, sometimes medical pay or PIP health policies tied to your automobile policy have non-reimbursement clauses, so you should pay attention to those when you can. You can find information on that in your automobile policy declaration sheet, also known as a "dec page." If you don't have a specific exclusion on these, you could argue *common fund doctrine* (see above) to try and negotiate a reduction on your own. However, if you have a good personal injury lawyer, he or she will do a great job on that argument.

WHAT ABOUT PUBLIC HEALTH INSURANCE? ·

If some or all of your medical care was covered under a public health plan, like Medicare, Medicaid or Medi-Cal (California), then rest assured you have both a statutory and contractual duty to communicate with them in regards to paying them back at the time of settlement. The reason is because your medical care involves public funds (both state and federal), and you maintain a higher duty of communicating with these entities. It's very strict, and lawyers in California, for example, are ethically bound to communicate with Medi-Cal! However, everything that has been discussed in this chapter is still available to you to argue for any reduction with or without a lawyer, but you'll need to check the law of the state in which you reside.

WHAT IS ERISA PROTECTION
ON MY HEALTH PLAN?

I'll keep this section very short because ERISA is extremely complicated. All you need to know as a consumer is that it's a federal law that governs some employee health plans, and it places limits on what you can do to fight your health insurance company when it comes to paying them back any money if you get in an accident. If your health plan is governed by ERISA, then it's said to be "ERISA protected." You can certainly find out on your own if your health plan has ERISA protection by looking at your SPD document. If ERISA is on your health plan, then you really should consider retaining a good injury lawyer if you haven't already. Remember, a skilled injury lawyer familiar with ERISA law will become a vital asset in negotiations when it comes time to reimburse your ERISA-protected health plan. The attorneys' fees can sometimes be usurped by the savings a knowledgeable ERISA plan lawyer can do for you on your injury case.

The next time you or your family get injured, and part or all of the medical care under some form of private or public health insurance is used, just be aware that reimbursement later to those entities may be necessary when you receive any settlement funds. However, the trick is understanding when state law protects you and when it doesn't. Not every injury case (like minor injuries) needs a lawyer, so this chapter has given you some insight and resources if you find yourself without a lawyer.

But for those who have moderate or severe injury cases, this chapter shows you the benefits of using a good injury lawyer and the power one can wield to fairly settle your case with your own health insurance company. So the next time you're shopping for the best attorney for your injury case, use this chapter to quiz him or her and what he or she expects to do when it comes time to reimburse your health plan.

About Mark

California trial lawyer and bestselling legal author, Mark C. Blane, specializes in personal injury law. As a prolific writer, he has written and published 10 books and is a member of the National Academy of Best-Selling Authors. He was born in Germany and raised in Louisiana, where he graduated from Louisiana State University in Shreveport with two degrees: one in psychology and the other in criminal justice. He earned a law degree from Thomas Jefferson School of Law in San Diego in December 1998. He has been admitted to the California, Minnesota and Texas state bars and various federal courts. Mark represents people in Southern California who've been injured by defective products, motor vehicle accidents, slip and falls, and the like. He fights against some of the largest insurance companies in the United States, and he speaks German, Spanish and Italian.

Mark recognized early in his career that he wanted to represent ordinary people instead of corporate interests. He enjoys the courtroom and understands the necessity of having jury trials available when needed to right the wrongs of those injured. By practicing personal injury law, he's able to combine his two passions: law and human anatomy science. He further understands that not every injury case will need a lawyer, but every injury case, should be discussed with good legal counsel.

His law office is primarily comprised of a team of paralegals, and one *Of Counsel* attorney member. He likes keeping his legal team small and approachable. He can be reached direct at (619) 813-7955. You can also find him on the web at www. blanelaw.com.

CHAPTER 13

3 Major Secrets the Insurance Company Doesn't Want You to Know About Your Personal Injury Claim:
A Former Insurance Company Lawyer Reveals All

By Gary Martin Hays

"Speak up for those who cannot speak up for themselves, for the rights of all who are destitute. Speak up and judge fairly; defend the rights of the poor and needy." ~ Proverbs 31: 8, 9

When a client enters my law firm, they see this quote from the Book of Proverbs in the Old Testament mounted by the front door. It's a mission statement for my law firm. As attorneys, it's a privilege to help our clients "right" their "wrongs," and not something we take lightly.

There's an old legal maxim: "Everyone has a right to an attorney."

At my firm, we live by this variation:

> "Everyone has a right to an attorney.
> However, they do not have the right
> to have MY LAW FIRM as their attorneys."

We must believe in our clients before we agree to accept the case. If we don't think they have a valid claim or are pursuing their case for the wrong reasons, we politely decline to represent them.

This wasn't always the case in my professional career. When I first started practicing law, I worked for a law firm that represented insurance companies. It was our job to defend people that caused automobile wrecks. We couldn't decline to represent someone unless there was a conflict of interest. Even if the defendant was driving drunk, plowed into a school bus full of kids, and had no remorse, we couldn't refuse to defend the case.

This experience working for insurance companies wasn't all bad or a waste of time, as I learned many valuable lessons. With more than 23 years of experience, I've learned a lot about personal injury claims. I want to give you a peek behind the curtain and share three major secrets the insurance companies don't want you to know.

SECRET #1: YOU'LL GET MORE MONEY FOR YOUR INJURY CLAIMS IF YOU HIRE AN ATTORNEY

Insurance adjusters are trained to act like your long-lost friend. They'll say, "You don't need an attorney! We're here to help. An attorney won't be able to get you more money." Please don't fall for this trick if you or a family member has been hurt in a wreck!

In 1999, a Consumer Panel Survey of Auto Accident Victims by the Insurance Research Council (IRC) tells a much different story insurers don't want you to know:

- Injured victims receive an average of *40 percent more money* just by consulting a lawyer to learn their rights.

- Injured victims receive an average of *three and a half times more money* before legal fees when they hire an attorney to defend their rights!

(Stats from 1999 IRC report "Paying for Auto Injuries")

The insurance company won't explain your *rights* to you. The insurer is also not going to explain their *responsibilities* to you. You need an attorney to analyze all potential causes of actions, as well as to help you understand who may be responsible for paying for your claims.

SECRET #2: INSURANCE COMPANIES PRACTICE THE 3 D'S WHEN HANDLING CLAIMS

What are the three D's?

- Delay
- Deny
- Defend

There are a few ways insurance companies make money. One is by charging premiums to keep the insurance in force. Another is by taking this money and investing it. I don't criticize these actions; insurers have every right to make money. But there's another way that insurers make money that *is* offensive: When an insurer treats the claims unit as a "profit center," this is wrong. Consider this example: You run a red light and cause a wreck, injuring the other driver. He looks to you to take care of his medical bills, lost wages, and pain and suffering. Your insurance company handles the calls and settles the claims against you. The negotiations at the insurance company are by the claims department. This department sets aside money, called "reserves," to settle claims.

How does the insurer turn their claims department into a profit center? By paying out less than what should be paid on the claim. This is done in three different ways:

1. *Delay:* The insurance company has the upper hand because they have the money. The injured victim needs money for medical bills or for lost wages. The paychecks stop coming, but the bills do not. When injured victims are bent over the financial barrel, the insurer knows they can get most people to accept less by delaying the claim.

2. *Deny:* If you submit a claim, the adjuster will allege:

   - You're faking your injuries.
   - You're exaggerating your injuries.
   - If you're hurt, it's because you were injured *before* the wreck.

- If you were really hurt, you should have chosen a "real" doctor.
- You overtreated for your injuries.
- If you've lost wages, it wasn't because of your injuries.

The adjuster never admits that your injuries or claims are due to the wreck. You're just a money-grubbing person seeking "life's lottery" from the insurer.

3. *Defend:* If you don't like the insurer's offer, or if the insurer denies your claim, you have three choices:

- drop your claim;
- accept the low offer; or
- file a lawsuit.

If you file a lawsuit, be prepared for the insurer to deny your claims and attack you. Unless it's a case of crystal-clear liability, the insurer will blame you for the wreck or apportion some fault to you. They'll use the courts to delay the claim. Further, be prepared to spend time and money with the lawsuit, and having your entire medical and work history scrutinized by the insurer's lawyers.

On February 7, 2007, CNN's Anderson Cooper wrote on his *360* blog "Insurance Companies Fight Paying Billions in Claims." He asks the reader to assume they're driving down the road when a truck runs into the side of your car, denting the passenger door. You're hurt, but you don't know the severity of your injuries. Your doctor diagnoses soft tissue injuries and whiplash, and sends you to therapy. You miss work, and end up with $15,000 in medical expenses and $10,000 in lost wages. You send a demand to the insurer and ask them to cover just your out-of-pocket expenses of $25,000. You expect the insurance company to do the right thing. But what do you do when the insurer only offers you $15,000 and says "take it or leave it"?

Cooper and his producer, Kathleen Johnston, investigated for 18 months how insurance companies were handling these "fender bender" claims. In particular, they researched how Allstate Insurance Company handled the claim of a woman from New Mexico. She had $25,000 in medical bills and lost wages, but Allstate only offered $15,000. Cooper wrote that "Martinez's case represents what 10 of the top 12 auto insurance companies are doing to save money. And if you're in a minor impact crash and get hurt, former insurance industry insiders say insurance companies will most likely try doing the same to you: Delay handling your claim, deny you were hurt, and defend their decision in drawn-out court battles. It's the three D's: delay, deny and defend." He added that this " 'is a strategy adopted by several major auto insurance companies over the past 10 years,' a lot of lawyers, former insurance company insiders, and others tell CNN."

These insurers are betting most people won't hire a lawyer and will accept the quick settlement offer to go away. Unfortunately, a lot of people do just that. What happens if you take that offer to settle without consulting an attorney? Once you sign that check and release, your claim is over. Some of the most difficult conversations I have with potential clients are when I have to explain to them there's nothing I can do because they waived all claims when they accepted the insurer's check. The adjuster convinced them they were just "sore" from the wreck and most people are fine in a couple of days. "There's no need to see a doctor or hire a lawyer as you will be wasting money," the adjuster told them. "I see this all the time. You'll be fine," she says in a reassuring tone. But the strain of the neck was really a herniated disk that needs surgical repair. The medical expenses alone could be over $50,000. The $500 settlement check that person accepted won't even cover the medications the person will need over the next six months. Unfortunately, there's nothing we can do to set aside the settlement. This happens over and over again—innocent people being taken advantage of by the insurance industry.

So how do you protect yourself?

SECRET #3: DON'T SIGN ANY PAPERS OR TALK TO THE INSURANCE COMPANY BEFORE CONSULTING AN ATTORNEY

Here's a quick list of reasons why:

- You could be signing a "Release of *all* claims" without realizing it! The adjuster can tell you they need you to sign a medical release to get copies of your bills and records, but it could also have language on the form that settles your claim. This could be considered a settlement of all claims because you're responsible for reading and understanding anything you sign!

- Another trick is to give you a release that will settle your property damage repairs. You want your car back because you're tired of driving the rental vehicle. "Just sign this release, and I'll have the repair facility release your vehicle. I'll throw in an extra $200 for your hassle." You think the adjuster is being very nice, so you sign the form. But beware, even some property damage releases contain language that could jeopardize other claims.

- The adjuster can ask you to tell her about all injuries in a recorded statement. You mention your neck because it hurts. You also mention your left arm. However, you don't say anything about your lower back because you assume it will quickly improve. Days go by and your back really starts to hurt. You experience numbness shooting down your leg. You seek treatment and find out you have a herniated disk. The doctor tells you that you may need surgery. What happens when you tell the insurer about your herniated disk? They'll replay the recorded statement that doesn't mention the lower back so they *deny* that part of your injury claim. You weren't trying to mislead anyone, or present a fraudulent claim. You didn't know the severity of your injury when you gave the recorded interview. Imagine how it would sound in front of a jury when the insurer's lawyer plays the recording made after the wreck. "I am doing ok. Just hurt my neck and arm." This could be a significant blow to your case!

- Never sign a blanket medical authorization that allows the insurer to get any medical records they want from any medical provider you've ever seen. Even if it is your *own* insurance company, you should limit their ability to collect medical records from medical providers you treated with just for the accident.

If you or a family member has been hurt in a wreck, please realize this important fact about the insurance company: The insurance adjuster that represents the person at fault for your wreck is out to save the insurance company money, *not* to give you the compensation you deserve.

HOW DO I AVOID BEING HURT FOR A SECOND TIME AFTER MY WRECK?

As a former insurance defense lawyer, I highly recommend discussing your case with an attorney *before* you talk to the insurer. You have nothing to lose by calling an attorney, but think of all you can lose if you don't!

About Gary

Gary Martin Hays is not only a successful lawyer but a nationally recognized safety advocate who educates families and children on issues ranging from bullying to internet safety to abduction prevention. He currently serves on the board of directors of the Elizabeth Smart Foundation. Gary has been seen on countless television stations, including ABC, CBS, NBC and FOX affiliates. He has appeared on more than 110 radio stations, including the Georgia News Network, discussing legal topics and providing safety tips to families. He hosts "Georgia Behind the Scenes" on the CW Atlanta TV Network and has been quoted in *USA Today,* the *Wall Street Journal*, and featured on more than 250 online sites, including Morningstar.com, CBS News' MoneyWatch.com, the Boston Globe, the Miami Herald, and The New York Daily News.

He's also co-author of the bestselling books *Trendsetters: The World's Leading Experts Reveal Top Trends to Help You Achieve Health, Wealth and Success, Champions: Knockout Strategies for Health, Wealth and Success,* and *Sold: The World's Leading Real Estate Experts Reveal the Secrets to Selling Your Home for Top Dollar In Record Time.*

Gary graduated from Emory University in 1986 with a B.A. degree in Political Science and a minor in Afro-American and African Studies. In 1989, he received his law degree from the Walter F. George School of Law of Mercer University in Macon, Georgia. His legal accomplishments include being a member of the prestigious Multi Million Dollar Advocate's Forum, a society limited to attorneys who have received a settlement or verdict of at least $2 million. He has been recognized in *Atlanta Magazine* as one of Georgia's top workers' compensation lawyers, as one of the Top 100 Trial Lawyers in Georgia by the American Trial Lawyers Association, and by Lawdragon as one of the leading Plaintiffs' Lawyers in America. His firm specializes in personal injury, wrongful death, workers' compensation and pharmaceutical claims. Since 1993, his firm has helped more than 27,000 victims and their families recover more than $235 million.

In 2008, Gary started the non-profit organization Keep Georgia Safe, with the mission to provide safety education and crime prevention training in Georgia. The organization has trained more than 80 state and local law enforcement officers in CART (Child Abduction Response Teams) so first responders will know what to do in the event a child is abducted in Georgia. Gary has completed Child Abduction Response Team training with the National Amber Alert program through the U.S. Department of Justice. He's a certified instructor in the radKIDS curriculum. His law firm has given away 1,000 bicycle helmets and 14 college scholarships.

To learn more about Gary Martin Hays, visit www.GaryMartinHays.com.
To find out more about Keep Georgia Safe, please visit
www.KeepGeorgiaSafe.org or call (770) 934-8000.

CHAPTER 14

The Living Trust Plus™: True Asset Protection

By Evan H. Farr
Certified Elder Law Attorney*

Rich, poor, or somewhere in between, 99 percent of Americans can't afford to ignore the potentially catastrophic costs of nursing home care and other types of long-term care, such as assisted living and in-home care. In fact, long-term care costs are so tremendously high that 70 percent of individuals become impoverished within one year of entering a nursing home. Chances are that someone close to you has lost their dignity and their life savings by winding up broke in a nursing home.

Another huge risk to the financial security of elders is the growing problem of elderly drivers causing car accidents and being subject to financially devastating lawsuits. Numerous car crashes involving elderly drivers have made headline news over the past decade.

It's easy to understand why true asset protection—asset protection that protects your assets from the risks of auto accidents, nursing home expenses, and other risks of ordinary life—is so important to the growing population of aging Americans.

* Certification is through the National Elder Law Foundation and approved by the American Bar Association. The Commonwealth of Virginia, and many other states, have no procedure for approving certifying organizations.

THE PROBLEM EXPRESSED IN NUMBERS

Consider the following statistics:

- About 70 percent of Americans who live to age 65 will need long-term care at some time in their lives, over 40 percent in a nursing home.[1]

- As of 2011, the national average cost of a private room in a nursing home was $239 per day, or $87,235 per year, and the national average cost of a semi-private room was $214 per day, or $78,110 per year,[2] reflecting nearly a 5 and 6 percent increase from the previous year.

- On average, someone age 65 today will need long-term care services for three years, women averaging longer than men. Twenty percent of Americans will need long-term care for more than five years.[3]

- Long-term care is not just needed by the elderly. A study by Unum, released in November 2008, found that 46 percent of its group long-term care claimants were under the age of 65 at the time of disability.[4]

- According to the U.S. Census Bureau, the population of those over 75 is growing to 31 million by 2028. With accident rates for drivers over the age of 65 higher than for any other group except teens, this large increase in senior drivers is likely to result in upwards of 10,000 senior-related auto accidents per year.

- Although approximately 85 percent of drivers have auto insurance, *only about 10 percent of the population have long-term care insurance.* The sad truth about long-term care insurance is that most people don't have it because by the time they think about getting it, they're already too old to afford it or qualify for it, or they have a medical condition that prevents approval.

---

1 "Market Survey of Long-Term Care Costs," October 2011. http://www.metlife.com/assets/cao/mmi/publications/studies/2011/mmi-market-survey-nursing-home-assisted-living-adult-day-services-costs.pdf.

2 "Market Survey of Long-Term Care Costs," October 2011. http://www.metlife.com/assets/cao/mmi/publications/studies/2011/mmi-market-survey-nursing-home-assisted-living-adult-day-services-costs.pdf.

3 National Clearinghouse for Long-Term Care Information. www.longtermcare.gov at www.longtermcare.gov/LTC/Main_Site/Understanding_Long_Term_Care/Basics/Basics.aspx#need.

4 Insurance Information Institute. www.iii.org/media/facts/statsbyissue/longtermcare.

If you're one of the 90 percent who hasn't purchased long-term care insurance, what are your options for paying for long-term care? The best time to address this question is when you go to your lawyer for estate planning. Unfortunately, a tragic lack of awareness exists: Most estate planning attorneys don't know what true asset protection requires, and the average American doesn't even know that the possibility for true asset protection exists. What you need is a qualified elder law attorney who understands that the best estate planning in the world is useless if you wind up spending all your assets to pay for nursing home or getting sued for driving into a crowded farmers market and killing 10 people. What you need is an attorney who's a member of the **Living Trust Plus™ National Network** (more on this later).

True asset protection is designed to protect your assets in such a way that you retain the greatest level of control over your assets as possible, but that your assets are shielded in a way so that they're protected from future creditors and so that you can obtain Medicaid—the social safety net that pays for nursing home and home-based long-term care for American citizens. Most important, long-term care paid for by the Medicaid program is legally required to be of the same quality as that of a private pay patient. If you or your spouse served in the military on active duty during a period of wartime, true asset protection is also designed so that you can obtain a tax-free income benefit called Veteran's Aid and Attendance to help you pay for in-home care or assisted living.

THE LIVING TRUST LIMITATION

Many people think they can protect their nest eggs through estate planning using a traditional revocable living trust. Although a revocable living trust does a good job of avoiding probate when properly established and funded, an enormous limitation of a revocable living trust is that it does *not* protect assets whatsoever from creditors or from the expenses of long-term care. In a moment I'll teach you about a special type of trust—the Living Trust Plus™ —that *does* protect your assets from general creditors and from the expenses of long-term care, but first let's make sure you understand what's meant by the term "long-term care."

WHAT'S LONG-TERM CARE?

Long-term care isn't a type of health care. Long-term care isn't synonymous with long-term care insurance. The term "long-term care" means the actual care that's required when someone needs assistance with activities of daily living (such as bathing, eating, dressing and going to the bathroom) or assistance with the instrumental activities of daily living (such as cooking, cleaning, taking care of household chores, paying bills, and taking care of pets), not quite the basic human needs but pretty essential for someone to be able to live independently on their own. Once you need help with these things, you need long-term care, though of course there are many varying levels of long-term care.

Many people need long-term care due to dementia. Almost everybody knows someone with Alzheimer's disease or some other form of dementia. Alzheimer's is the third leading cause of death in this country. Of course, before it causes death, it causes people to lose the ability to handle their own activities of daily living. Some victims of Alzheimer's have physical problems, but many have simply lost their memory and their higher cognitive functions; they have forgotten how to eat, bathe, dress, brush their teeth, and do anything else to care for themselves. They might be able to do these things with somebody standing next to them and guiding them every step of the way, but they wouldn't be able to do anything if they didn't have constant supervision and reminders.

THE LIVING TRUST PLUS™ SOLUTION

Earlier I explained that a huge limitation of a revocable living trust is that it doesn't protect assets whatsoever from creditors or from the expenses of long-term care. In response to this weakness that's inherent with revocable living trusts, I developed a unique solution—a special type of asset protection trust called the Living Trust Plus™. Although it functions very similarly to a revocable living trust and maintains much of same flexibility, the Living Trust Plus™ is designed specifically to protect assets from the nightmare of probate, *plus* the expenses of long-term care, *plus* the dangers of car accidents and other general creditors.

I created Living Trust Plus™ about five years ago, and it's now being used by dozens of exceptional estate planning and elder law attorneys throughout the country, all of whom can be found listed on the website www.LivingTrustPlus.com. For purposes of Medicaid eligibility, the Living Trust Plus™ is the *only* type of asset protection trust that allows you to retain an interest in the trust while also protecting your assets from being counted against you by state Medicaid agencies.

The Living Trust Plus™ is an irrevocable asset protection trust that you create as part of your estate planning. The Living Trust Plus™ allows you to receive all ordinary income from the trust financial assets and to use any trust-owned realty or tangible personal property. The only restriction of the Living Trust Plus™ is you can have no direct access to principal. If either you or your spouse has direct access to principal, the assets in the trust would be deemed "countable" for Medicaid eligibility purposes and would be completely available to all other creditors. Prohibiting direct access to principal is the key to why the Living Trust Plus™ works. Because you can't withdraw principal, neither may your creditors. Despite this restriction, you have the ability to retain a very high degree of control over the Living Trust Plus™ assets. In addition to receiving all ordinary income from the trust, you can:

- Live in and use any trust-owned real estate.
- Sell any trust-owned real estate and have the trust purchase replacement real estate if desired.
- Use all trust-owned tangible personal property.
- Sell any trust-owned tangibles and have the trust purchase replacements if desired.
- Drive any trust-owned vehicles.
- Sell any trust-owned vehicles and have the trust purchase replacements if desired.

Additionally, you can:

- Serve as trustee of the Living Trust Plus™ if desired.
- Remove and replace someone else who's serving as trustee of the Living Trust Plus™.
- Change beneficiaries of the Living Trust Plus™ at any time during your life.

Although the Living Trust Plus™ is technically an "irrevocable" trust, this only means that you cannot unilaterally revoke the trust. Despite the fact that the trust is irrevocable, it can still be terminated so long as the trustee and all beneficiaries agree to terminate it. Many people, including many misinformed attorneys, erroneously think that the term "irrevocable" means the trust can never be revoked. But the fact is that the term "irrevocable" means just one thing—that the trust cannot be unilaterally revoked by the trust creator. Although the Living Trust Plus™ is irrevocable and can't be revoked unilaterally by the trust creator, under common law and under the Uniform Trust Code, this type of irrevocable trust can be modified, revoked or partially revoked upon the consent of all interested parties, which is the trust creator, the trustee, and all trust beneficiaries.

Although direct withdrawal of principal from the Living Trust Plus™ is prohibited, there's the potential to indirectly access the trust principal in two ways. The first way is that the trustee has the ability to make distributions of principal to the trust beneficiaries, who are typically your adult children. If the trustee distributes principal to a trust beneficiary, that beneficiary can then voluntarily return some or all of that principal or use some or all of that principal for your benefit. The second way for the settlor to possibly get at the trust principal is for the trust to be terminated by the agreement of all interested parties as just explained.

The main types of assets that can be protected using the Living Trust Plus™ are real estate, including your primary residence, financial investments, ordinary bank accounts, and any life insurance that has cash value. Qualified retirement plans can't be owned by a trust, so to be protected they must first be liquidated and subjected to taxation. The Living Trust Plus™ doesn't affect your retirement income or your primary checking account.

PROTECT YOUR RAINY DAY FUND

We live during a time when many baby boomers are taking care of their own parents and children, and consequently putting off planning for their own retirement and long-term care solutions. Furthermore, there are many Americans who can't qualify for long-term care insurance, and these are the ideal candidates for use of the true asset protection capabilities embodied by the Living Trust Plus™ Asset Protection Trust.

The typical clients who use the Living Trust Plus™ are in their mid-60s to mid-80s, already retired, and worried about the potential catastrophic cost of long-term care. They want to protect the nest egg that they've been saving for a rainy day.

Of course, as a certified elder law attorney, I know that the rainiest day possible is the day you wind up in a nursing home, so if you want to truly protect your nest egg and have it actually benefit you when the time comes,[5] you need to do something to protect that money. For the vast majority of Americans, the Living Trust Plus™ is the best way to get this much-needed protection.

---

5 The Living Trust Plus™ can benefit you because your children can voluntarily use the trust assets to supplement your care or purchase items not covered by Medicaid, thereby making your life more comfortable and dignified.

About Evan

Evan Farr is a certified elder law attorney and is widely recognized as one of the nation's leading experts in the fields of Medicaid Asset Protection and Medicaid trusts. Evan is the principal attorney of the Farr Law Firm, an elder law firm serving Virginia, Maryland and Washington, DC, and dedicated to helping protect seniors and their families by preserving dignity, quality of life and financial security. Evan has been named by *Virginia Super Lawyers* magazine as one of the top 5 percent of attorneys in Virginia since 2007, and by *Washington, DC, Super Lawyers* magazine as one of the top 5 percent of attorneys in DC since 2008. In 2011, Evan was named by *Washingtonian* magazine as one of the top attorneys in the Washington, DC, Metropolitan area, and was named in *Newsweek* magazine as one of the top attorneys in the country.

A nationally known author and continuing legal education speaker, Evan Farr has educated tens of thousands of attorneys across the country through speaking and writing for numerous national legal organizations, including ALI-ABA, the National Academy of Elder Law Attorneys, the National Business Institute, and the National Constitution Center, as well as his own Elder Law Institute for Training and Education (ELITE), through which he coaches and trains other elder law attorneys around the country, providing them with specialized software and practice-enhancement systems, such as the Living Trust Plus™ Asset Protection System used by dozens of attorneys across the nation. Evan is also a well-known public media figure, having been quoted or cited as an elder law expert by the *Washington Post, Newsweek magazine, Northern Virginia Magazine, Trusts & Estates* magazine, the American Institute of Certified Public Accountants, and the American Bar Association, and has appeared on television on PBS, MSNBC, Fox News, and CNN.

To learn more about Evan Farr, creator of the Living Trust Plus™ Asset Protection Trust and to learn how you can legally and ethically protect you or your client's assets from nursing home expenses, visit the Living Trust Plus™ website at www.LivingTrustPlus.com, the Farr Law Firm's website at www.FarrLawFirm.com, or call toll-free (800) 399-FARR.

CHAPTER 15

Asset Protection for Real Estate Pros

By Mark Torok, Esq.

No doubt about it. The landscape for real estate professionals has undergone a seismic shift in the last few years. Gone are the days when mortgage lenders offered easy terms to anyone who could fog a mirror, when a property sold for above listing price in a matter of hours, when every house was sold through a licensed real estate agent, and when real estate investors could be assured of making a huge profit on a property just by waiting a few months to sell. And with some estimating that 89 percent of today's real estate agents will leave the business by the beginning of 2013, those who are left will be even more in the lawyers' crosshairs as the maze of statutes, regulations and judge-made law continues to multiply exponentially.

Real estate pros, now more than ever, need to be aware of their exposure to lawsuits and their ability to protect their assets from the very beginning of their careers. The principles of the use of insurance, disclosures and the tactical use of entities can effectively allow real estate pros to operate in markets today and in coming years, free of the uncertainty that a lawsuit (or two) will wipe them out financially and emotionally.

5 ELEMENTS OF AN ASSET PROTECTION PLAN

Every asset protection plan should contain five elements:

1. *Every real estate pro should engage in their activities with honesty and integrity.* While this seems to be so obvious as to seem trite, it's surprising how many real estate pros forget this simple principle when faced with a tough question or situation.

2. *Every asset protection plan should be simple, reasonable, easy to administer, and explainable to the average person in three minutes or less.*

3. *Every asset protection plan has to be legal and legitimate.* You don't want to explain to the jury that the reason you incorporated in Nevada was to hide yourself from the eyes of the public or that you set up a byzantine maze of companies to hide your true identity.

4. *Every asset protection plan must protect against financial ruin.* No asset protection plan can protect against every lawsuit or every action. If a person intentionally does something wrong or acts negligently, however well-intentioned, that causes harm to another, *no* court is going to protect all your assets in the event you do something wrong and someone is seriously hurt by your actions (or inactions). The most you could expect of a good asset protection plan is to protect against total financial ruin.

5. *Every good asset protection plan should take into account estate planning and tax considerations.* There are many benefits to real estate investing and our tax code and estate planning laws are set up to provide significant benefits to real estate and real estate investing.

3 LEGS OF A GOOD ASSET PROTECTION PLAN

There are three legs to a good asset protection plan for the real estate pro: insurance, disclosures, and the proper selection and use of entities.

Insurance

Insurance against losses is one of the basic supports of our modern society and business. Without insurance, investors and businesspeople wouldn't risk doing business if a catastrophe could wipe out their livelihood in minutes. Insurance allows for buildings to be built and land developed, businesses to operate and lenders to lend.

In addition to property insurance that protects hard assets against loss from certain causes (or perils),[1] business liability insurance (called a commercial general liability policy, or CGL), protects your assets in the event of a lawsuit over something you did (or didn't do).

While it's true that insurance policies don't cover all perils[2], liability insurance is critical because it covers defense costs. If an examination of the lawsuit documents reveals that a claim might be covered, an insurer must defend the entire suit. The ability to have defense costs paid by the insurer cannot be overstated. In fact, a client recently drove this home in a unique way:

One of my clients, Mike,[3] called my office and asked me whether it was too late to get the liability insurance I had mentioned in a presentation given to the local real estate investors association a few months before. He related that he had received a call from a gentleman who had a house that he wanted to get rid of, if Mike could convince the resident that had defaulted on the contract for deed to vacate the premises.

Mike went to the property, knocked on the door, introduced himself, and indicated he was there to see if they would vacate the house and turn it back over to the owner, since they weren't making the payments and were going to lose the house anyway. The resident slammed the door in his face and told him to go away.

Mike did so, reported his encounter with the resident, and let the matter drop.

Several months later, Mike and the homeowner were served with a lawsuit alleging that he caused emotional distress to the resident. Of course, the suit was dubious at best, and that's why Mike called my office.

Unfortunately, Mike was out of luck as far as getting insurance to cover this lawsuit.

Mike had to bear the costs of defending himself and was able to get

---

1 Property insurance covers hard assets from loss due to destruction of the property by a covered peril or cause. It replaces buildings when they burn down or personal property when it is stolen, for example.
2 Generally the perils that aren't covered under a policy are for intentionally caused losses as well as those perils that are too severe to cover, such as flood or windstorm.
3 The name of the client has been changed to protect his identity.

himself extricated from the suit on summary judgment, but it cost him almost $17,000 in legal fees. Given that a CGL policy would have cost Mike less than $1,000 in premiums for a million dollars in coverage for a year (with a reasonable deductible) and would have covered his attorney fees, Mike's failure to get insurance for his business cost him a lot in time, stress and money for something that turned out to be an innocent inquiry.

For real estate pros, liability coverage is critical. Most real estate brokers have errors and omissions coverage (E&O) that protects them against losses caused by their agents in the course of business, but landlords and real estate investors also critically need liability coverage for their land-lording operations (slips and falls and other losses) and property coverage to protect against physical loss of the property. Given the relatively low coverage cost, it's a foolish decision to operate without liability coverage (with provisions for defense costs!). A competent insurance agent will be more than willing to provide additional information on protecting yourself with insurance.

Disclosures

The second leg of the asset protection stool is the appropriate use of disclosures in a transaction. Most state real estate commissions, realtor boards and even some legislatures have done a fairly good job of preparing or mandating certain disclosures and forms in real estate transactions. Most real estate professionals are (or should be) very aware as to what to say and not to say about a particular situation to be legally compliant. It's common for regulators to require a written description of the relationship between the agent and home buyer or seller, the condition of the property, and certain other disclosures (such as information about tidelands, farming lands, earthquake zones, radon, child molesters, etc.)

The effective use of disclosures, in which "material" facts are disclosed to the parties, is critical to avoiding lawsuits down the road. The prudent course is to disclose anything that a "reasonable" person would consider important in making a decision about the property. In practice, such disclosures don't usually result in the loss of the deal, but if it does, be thankful you disclosed it, because if you hadn't, the money you would have made from the deal would certainly pale in comparison to the aggravation, time and money spent to defend yourself later.

Proper Use of Entities

The final leg of the asset protection stool is the proper use of entities. The creation and use of entities is what people think of most when they think of asset protection, and it's a critical part of any plan.

The use of separate entities is based on the old adage "don't put all your eggs in one basket." When I present this concept to audiences, I used to actually use four real eggs in one basket to illustrate that if one of the eggs (representing a property) were to go bad, the others would crash as well. I would then drop the basket, and the eggs would all break. Next, I would put several single eggs in their own baskets and drop one basket (usually the egg would break) and demonstrate that I could still eat with the other eggs in the other separate baskets. This proved to be a successful demonstration until one day the plastic bag containing the eggs broke along with the eggs, splattering the first two rows of the audience with raw egg![4]

The types of available vehicles in which to do business in the United States have exploded in the last two or three decades, as legislatures respond to the increasing complexities of modern business and the demands of entrepreneurs. Previously, you could set up your business as a sole proprietor, a general partnership, a joint venture, a limited partnership or a corporation. Today, in addition to these vehicles, we now have limited liability companies, C corporations and S corporations, limited liability partnerships, limited liability limited partnerships, real estate investment trusts, other trusts, and other accounts (such as retirement accounts) that all offer some protection against creditors' claims. Even bankruptcy courts are being used as a shield these days.

For small to medium-sized real estate entrepreneurs, we usually only recommend one or two of three types: trusts, corporations and/or limited liability companies.[5]

Trusts have been touted by other gurus as the best thing since sliced bread for real estate investors over the last decade. However, there has been a backlash against the use of trusts, and in some states, a trust isn't

---

4 If I were a (bad) vaudevillian comedian, I would suggest that I really had egg on my face that day! (Cymbal crash and rim shot here please.)

5 We've often used limited partnerships and other types of entities in the past, but generally with the strengthening of the laws with respect to limited liability companies, we more often than not recommend them to our clients.

even considered a separate entity,[6] which obviously offers little, if any, protection for the assets held in the trust. However, in some states, trusts are legislatively authorized or court approved and can provide excellent asset protection for properties located in those states.[7]

Corporations are useful as property-holding entities and offer excellent asset protection. The "double tax" consequences of being taxed as a corporation (15 percent on the first $50,000 and 35 percent on income after that) and again on dividend distributions

can be addressed through the use of an S corp, with its pass-through taxation of income.[8]

In most instances, though, the modern-day limited liability company is the vehicle of choice for real estate pros in today's business world. An LLC offers most of the attributes of a corporation, such as centralized management and perpetual life, but also allows for pass-through taxation (like a partnership), and offers superior asset protection for investors because of the "charging order."

Unlike corporations in which a creditor can seize the stock certificates and take over the rights of the owner's shares (i.e., vote the shares, sell them, etc), in an LLC, the creditor is only entitled to obtain a charging order from the court, which allows the creditor to receive only the distributions the debtor would receive. If the person doesn't get a distribution, neither does the creditor. The creditor doesn't get to seize the membership units or vote the units. Instead, all the creditor will get is the right to receive whatever the member receives by way of distribution from the LLC, which is usually nothing, leaving the LLC untouched.[9]

If you're using different exit strategies with respect to real estate investing, you'll want to isolate your "flipping" business from your rental

---

6 Texas is the most populated state to deny trusts a "separate entity status." See in re: The Ray Maloolly Trust, TX Supreme Ct, 2006.

7 The six states that have been statutorily authorized are: Illinois, Florida, Hawaii, North Dakota, Virginia and Georgia .

8 Note though that an S corporation has its own requirements as well that could limit its effectiveness in certain circumstances. For example, an S corp must be held by individuals, have a calendar year tax year, cannot be owned by more than 35 persons, etc.

9 Some have even suggested that if the judgment debtor owes taxes on the LLC's non-distributed income, that the creditor with a charging order may be stuck with a tax bill without receiving any funds at all. It's unlikely this would happen if the judgment creditor has competent counsel.

properties, not only because of the different risks in each segment but also for tax reasons. When an investor flips properties, the IRS will consider that investor a "dealer."[10] If you're tagged with the dealer label, you aren't considered to be an investor, and all your properties are considered inventory. You won't be able to take depreciation deductions for your properties, nor will you get long-term capital gains treatment when you sell the property.

By the use of entities separating your long-term holds from your dealer properties, you can shield your tax benefits on your long-term holdings from the tax consequences of dealer status. We usually advise the use of multiple entities (corporations and LLCs) to effectively isolate business segments and to segregate the real estate pro's assets.

For the real estate pro, protection from financial ruin and unscrupulous attorneys who prey on the uninformed must be a priority, but it doesn't need to be complicated. Insurance (property and liability), good disclosures, and the effective use of entities to segregate assets and provide substantial tax advantages are well worth the minimal time necessary to establish and maintain to be protected.

---

10 Factors that go into determining dealer status include the duration of ownership (two years is usually safe); your manifestations of intent at the time you bought the property (did you immediately put it up for sale?); the extent and nature of your efforts to sell the property; the number, substance and continuity of your sales (do you do this repeatedly?); the use of a business office for the sale of your property; and the time and effort you devote to sales.

About Mark

Mark Torok is the "Master of Real Estate Investing." He began his legal career in Washington in 1983 and is licensed to practice law in Texas and Pennsylvania as well. He's the founder of The Torok Law Firm PC, a law firm dedicated to representing real estate investors and small-business owners, and creating innovative, unique legal solutions for his clients in real estate, securities, estate planning, and protecting and preserving their wealth and assets. He and his firm have been involved in more than 700 transactions/closings in the past two years (the vast majority using non-traditional, creative financing techniques), and he represents some of the largest investors in Texas and throughout the United States. He's an active real estate investor and currently owns close to 800 units of various types in and around Texas. He holds a real estate salesperson's license, state bar admissions, an escrow officer license, and has a close relationship with Providence Title Co., which provides superior tile services. He has been an administrative law judge, represented a national trade association, and has been securities counsel and compliance officer for several companies.

He's also a principal in Torok Law Education Co., a firm dedicated to guiding investors through the world of real estate investing and asset protection, with classes and training products covering the legal side of real estate investments.

Mark is an active speaker throughout the United States and has presented seminars, boot camps, and talks on real estate, asset protection and federal and state laws, including mortgage assignment, lease options, contract for deed, the SAFE Act, the MARS Act, Dodd-Frank, Garn-St. Germain, and the myths (and truths) about other guru's programs.

To contact his firm or learn more about the programs offered, please call (210) 408-0050, or visit www.toroklaw.com.

CHAPTER 16

7 Things You *Must* Know About Dangerous Pharmaceutical Drugs

By Brad Lakin, Esq.

When taking any prescription medication, you should be an informed consumer. Take a proactive approach by first talking with your physician and conducting your own due diligence. This chapter will give you a good starting point. Following are seven things you should know about pharmaceutical drugs.

1. PHARMACEUTICAL DRUGS ARE TOXIC

It usually begins with a phone call or a visit from a client. Frustrated, concerned and confused, they've just learned that their life-altering or life-threatening medical condition may be caused by a dangerous drug. Unbeknownst to them, the pharmaceutical company failed to disclose the harmful side effects of the drug that were discovered by the company during testing. They're shocked to learn that the information about the drug's negative side effects was never released to the FDA during the drug's approval process. Unfortunately, the toxic side effects and dangers associated with this prescription drug were not known until it was too late.

We rarely think of prescription drugs as toxins, but all pharmaceutical drugs are synthetically engineered toxins. While some have proved to be quite effective, many have caused severe life-changing injuries, and in some cases death. The toxicity of pharmaceuticals is best described by Dr. Steven Hotze who's a sought-after health and wellness expert and is increasingly called upon to develop programs that address underlying problems without masking them with pharmaceuticals. "Remember, drugs are chemical molecules that never existed before in nature, and the body has to detoxify them, and they have to be detoxified by the liver," says Hotze.[1] He goes on to explain that a toxin is a poison—that all drugs are poison.

2. FDA APPROVAL GIVES CONSUMERS A FALSE SENSE OF SAFETY

Most consumers develop a false sense of safety, assuming the drug must be safe, or it would never have been approved by the FDA. Unfortunately, numerous FDA-approved drugs have been proved to be dangerous. The anti-inflammatory drug Vioxx, for example, killed more than 240,000 people. Several thousand people die a year from taking Tylenol.[2] Yes, Tylenol! In fact, in 2011, Tylenol decreased the daily maximum dosage in an effort to prevent accidental deaths from overdose. [3] It's important to understand that the FDA doesn't do its own testing; they rely on the pharmaceutical company's testing. Statistics concerning fatalities from drugs are quite staggering.

3. PHARMACEUTICAL DRUGS ARE THE 4TH LEADING CAUSE OF DEATH

The *Journal of the American Medical Association* (JAMA) published a study regarding prescription drug fatalities in U.S. hospitals. The study was conducted on adverse drug reactions (ADR). According to the study, data from U.S. Hospitals from 1966 to 1996 was analyzed. It found that prescription drugs were the fourth leading cause of all U.S. deaths. A total of 106,000 persons die every year from ADRs. Fatalities from ADRs are only superseded by heart disease, cancer and stroke, respectively. A recent newspaper article, using statistics from a 2009

1 Dr. Steven Hotze. Hotze Health & Wellness Center, 20214 Braidwood Dr., #215, Houston, TX 77450. www.hotzehwc.com.

2 "Great Day Houston." "Dr. Hotze-Potential Dangers of Pharmaceutical Drugs." "Great Day Houston." Web. August 10, 2009. http://www.youtube.com/watch?v=K6vbTPz_EcU.

3 www.medicalnewstoday.com. July 28, 2011.

study, counts deaths from ADRs so numerous that they exceed motor vehicle accident fatalities.[4]

The potential tremendous harm isn't limited to prescription drugs. As previously referenced, Tylenol has been linked to severe liver problems. Problems with Tylenol are so significant that the FDA convened a two-day meeting of its advisory committee on the subject. On the Q&A section of its website, Tylenol answers the question "Are there risks from taking too much acetaminophen (the generic name of the drug)?" with the statement that serious liver damage is possible if one takes too much.[5] Symptoms of liver damage, or overdose, include abdominal pain, appetite loss, coma, convulsions, diarrhea, irritability, jaundice, nausea, sweating, upset stomach and vomiting. Whether prescription drugs or over-the-counter medicines, numerous factors can coalesce to result in life-altering injuries and/or death.

4. PHARMACEUTICALS INJURE AND KILL

The *Wall Street Journal*'s "Market Watch" compiled a list of the 10 worst drug recalls in the history of the FDA. Their research was based on data from the U.S. Department of Justice and LexisNexis. Historical examples of drug recalls reveal the magnitude of injury caused to those who took these medications and the reprehensible conduct of pharmaceutical companies in response. In some cases, settlements included admissions of "intent to defraud or mislead." In the case of Bextra, it resulted in the largest fine ever imposed ($1.2 billion), plus monetary damages in civil litigation. Bextra was alleged to have caused, among other things, a fatal skin condition. Vioxx was an anti-inflammatory with dangerous side effects that included the increased risk of heart attack and stroke.

While Bextra set records for criminal penalties, Vioxx tops the chart for being the largest drug recall in history. The public reaction was unprecedented. U.S. awards against the manufacturer Merck were $4.8 billion, with an additional $1 billion in legal fees.[6] In the first case tried against Merck, the jury deliberated less than 11 hours. The widow of Robert Ernst, a Texas triathlete, was awarded $253.4 million in punitive and

---

4 Lisa Girion, Scott Glover, Doug Smith. Los Angeles Times. September 17, 2011.
5 http://www.fda.gov/forconsumers/consumerupdates/ucm168830.htm
6 *Wall Street Journal* "Market Watch." "The Ten Worst Drug Recalls in the History of the FDA." December 10, 2010.

compensatory damages.[7]

In a much smaller, but similarly interesting case, the diabetes drug Rezulin was eventually removed from the market after much delay by the FDA. The supposition was that the makers of Rezulin exerted a great deal of pressure on the agency. In the end, however, a number of the Able Laboratories managers were convicted of fraudulently distributing misbranded and adulterated drugs. Able Labs went out of business.[8]

Fen-Phen, a meteorically popular drug for weight loss, amassed awards and legal fees that totaled $21 billion. Those taking the drug experienced heart disease and other pulmonary-related disorders. More than 50,000 people sued Wyeth, the maker of the drug.

These are just a few examples of past recalls. The list of dangerous drugs and their adverse side effects literally goes on and on.

5. PHARMACEUTICAL COMPANIES OFTEN MISLEAD THE FDA DURING THE DRUG APPROVAL PROCESS

The FDA drug approval process isn't without criticism. For years, the FDA has been questioned about the influence that Big Pharma's special-interest lobbying efforts have had on them. In more recent years, the FDA has taken a more aggressive and progressive approach to investigating pharmaceuticals. While the process is fairly simple to understand in theory, it has become long, costly (some contend prohibitively so), and embroiled in controversy from nearly every perspective.

The U.S. FDA's Center for Drug Evaluation and Research (CDER) is charged with evaluating new drugs. The process is lengthy and is comprised of numerous steps and summarized by the FDA as follows:

1. Preclinical (animal) testing

2. An investigational new drug application (IND) outlines what the sponsor of a new drug proposes for human testing in clinical trials.

3. Phase 1 studies (typically involve 20 to 80 people)

---

7 Kaufman, Marc. Jury Faults Maker of Vioxx in Death of Texas Triathlete. *Washington Post.* Saturday, August 20, 2005.

8 *Wall Street Journal* "Market Watch." "The Ten Worst Drug Recalls in the History of the FDA." December 10, 2010.

4. Phase 2 studies (typically involve a few dozen to about 300 people)

5. Phase 3 studies (typically involve several hundred to about 3,000 people)

6. The pre-NDA period, just before a new drug application (NDA) is submitted; a common time for the FDA and drug sponsors to meet

7. Submission of an NDA is the formal step asking the FDA to consider a drug for marketing approval.

8. After an NDA is received, the FDA has 60 days to decide whether to file it so it can be reviewed.

9. If the FDA files the NDA, an FDA review team is assigned to evaluate the sponsor's research on the drug's safety and effectiveness.

10. The FDA reviews information that goes on a drug's professional labeling (information on how to use the drug).

11. The FDA inspects the facilities where the drug will be manufactured as part of the approval process.

12. FDA reviewers will approve the application or issue a complete response letter.[9]

Because the FDA relies only on the data provided by the drug company, history is replete with examples of dangerous side effects and data being hidden from the FDA during the approval process.

6. BIG PHARMA GREED GOES GLOBAL WHILE GETTING FAT FROM ADVERTISING

Global pharmaceutical sales exceed $800 million[10] due in no small part to the pervasiveness of drug ads. If you watch television, you watch pharmaceutical advertisements. What is the result of all this spending and watching? Studies suggest that pharmaceutical companies are profiting big time. A study conducted by The Kaiser Family Foundation found "a yield of an additional $4.20 in sales for every dollar spent on direct-to-consumer advertising."[11] Drug companies also spend twice as much on marketing (in the United States) as they do on research and development,

---

9 www.fda.gov

10 www.dailyfinance.com. "Global Pharmaceutical Sales Expected to Rise to $880 Million in 2001." October 10, 2010.

11 Meredith B. Rosenthal, Ernst R. Berndt, Julie M. Donohue, Arnold M. Epstein, and Richard G. Frank. "Demand Effects of Recent Changes in Prescription Drug Promotion" (Menlo Park, CA: The Kaiser Family Foundation, June 2003). pp. 18-19.

a disturbing fact to say the least.[12] Big Pharma's ability to spend more on advertising is directly related to their ability to reduce costs by moving manufacturing facilities overseas.

In domestic communities where pharmaceutical manufacturing plants were located, initial concerns developed over jobs being lost overseas to foreign manufacturing facilities. More recently, additional concerns have developed over quality control and

even national security. When Bristol-Myers Squibb closed its factory in East Syracuse, New York, in 2004, it was the last in the country to manufacture key components used in antibiotics, namely penicillin. According to a 2009 article in *The New York Times*, Senator Sherrod Brown (D-OH) said, "The lack of regulation around outsourcing is a blind spot that leaves room for supply disruptions, counterfeit medicines, even bioterrorism."[13] Drug companies that choose to move their operations abroad do so largely for the same reasons manufactures of other products do: less regulation, fewer environmental concerns, and a reduced cost of labor and construction.

All these factors bring about concern over quality control in global drug manufacturing facilities. The World Health Organization has a 300-plus page document called *Quality Assurance of Pharmaceutical*, which includes chapters on good manufacturing practices, starting materials, inspections, hazard and risk analysis, and sampling operations. However, with all the policy and protections in place, a crisis with tainted Heparin was linked to the death of at least 81 Americans and hundreds of serious adverse effects. Heparin was an anticoagulant drug used in cancer patients. After much investigation, the culprit for "bad" Heparin components was found to be the Chinese manufacturing facility.

Big Pharma advertising and moving drug manufacturing facilities abroad has been detrimental to consumers. More consumers end up taking pharmaceuticals that often lead to severe, adverse consequences as a result of relaxed safety regulations and poor quality control in foreign manufacturing facilities.

---

12 Gagnon, M. A. and Lexchin, J. "The Cost of Pushing Pills: A New Estimate of Pharmaceutical Promotion Expenditures in the United States." *PloS Medicine*. January 2008.

13 "Drug Making's Move Abroad Stirs Concerns." Gardiner Harris. *The New York Times*. January 19, 2009.

7. HOW TO BEST PROTECT YOURSELF
AND YOUR FAMILY

Knowledge is power, and there's an abundance of it available. Of course, there's nothing you can do to protect yourself and your family from greedy pharmaceutical companies that withhold data about dangerous prescription drugs. But, there are a number of resources that can quickly bring you up to speed on the status of drugs that may be faulty, have dangerous side effects, or are recalled. Here are four great resources:

1. *FDA (www.fda.gov):* The website lists not only drugs that have been recalled but medical devices as well. The list is compiled in date order with the most recent recalls listed first.

2. *FDA App:* The FDA has taken notification to a new level by creating an application for Android mobile phones, called Recalls. gov. This app is only available as a download at USA.gov. Type the following link into your browser to navigate directly to this page: http://apps.usa.gov/product-recalls-2/

3. *Physicians' Desk Reference (www.pdr.net):* This book is published annually for physicians and is also available on CD-ROM, at libraries and in bookstores. It contains manufacturers' prescribing information that's available to consumers in the form of package inserts. The "Drug Alert" tab is perhaps the best feature.

4. *National Patient Safety Foundation (www.npsf.org):* It's mission is "to improve the safety of patients by identifying and creating a core body of knowledge, identifying pathways to apply the knowledge, developing and enhancing the culture of receptivity to patient safety, raising public awareness, and foster communications about patient safety and improving the status of the foundation and its ability to meet its goals." A comprehensive list of organizations that provide an information infrastructure for safer health care can be found on its website.[14]

Consumers should take a proactive approach when contemplating taking prescription medications by talking to their physician and conducting research. For those who have already fallen victim to Big Pharma's dangerous drugs, pursuing a legal claim is often the only recourse. If

---

14 http://www.npsf.org/for-patients-consumers/links-and-further-reading/

you're confronted with this situation, make sure you're dealing with a law firm that has the knowledge and experience to successfully represent you against the pharmaceutical company.

About Brad

Brad Lakin, Esq. is a bestselling author and trial lawyer who is often sought out by media to discuss his clients' cases. Brad has appeared on ABC, CBS, NBC, FOX affiliates and CNN as well as being quoted and written about in newspapers throughout the country. Brad has repeatedly been recognized by his peers as a *Super Lawyer*, a *Rising Star,* and in 2006 as one of *Forty Lawyers Under Forty to Watch.* He has also been honored as a *Top 100 Trial Lawyer* by the National Trial Lawyers, a nationwide organization. These honors stem from his success as a litigator in the courtroom.

In a 2005 product liability trial, Lakin helped his clients win a $43 million victory—the second largest verdict ever in Illinois and the 30th nationwide. The case was a featured story throughout the country and included an appearance on CNN's "Anderson Cooper 360." Brad has tried cases to verdict in Illinois, Oklahoma, Arkansas, West Virginia, Nebraska, Missouri and Ohio. During the course of his career, his firm has represented clients in all 50 states.

Brad is known nationally for his successful courtroom advocacy in personal injury, mass torts, and a variety of complex litigation matters. His firm has recovered more than $700 million in verdicts, settlements and benefits for their clients. To learn more about Brad Lakin and his firm, visit www.GreatInjuryLawyers.com, or call (800) 851-5523.

CHAPTER 17

Are You Protecting Your Family's Way of Life? A Guide to Buying Insurance

By Damon Pendleton, Esq.

Let's face it, the average American family works hard for everything they get. Life requires it. Nothing is given. When you work hard to acquire nice things in life for you and your family, you definitely want to protect and defend them from others who may threaten your way of life. A significant part of protecting yourself and your family involves a comprehensive insurance plan. However, if you're like most people, you don't know what *type* of insurance or the appropriate *amount* to purchase. If so, that's completely normal so don't feel embarrassed. We'll explore some of your options from an attorney's point of view, not an insurance guy trying to sell you something.

First, I'll share a true story about a family I recently represented in a wrongful death case. I believe this story perfectly illustrates why every family needs to work with professionals to determine the appropriate insurance for them.

I've changed the names for privacy reasons, but the facts are absolutely true. Sadly, situations just like this one arise each and every day across our country. No person can foresee misfortune, but smart households owe it to their loved ones and themselves to be prepared for misfortune should it occur. Don't let this happen to your family.

MARY'S FAMILY STORY

Mary, a wife and mother, was excited because after months of searching for a new position she had just accepted a job offer with her new employer. Mary lived in the city, so she normally used mass transit to get around town. This particular Wednesday a casual friend (we'll call him John) drove by Mary's place to show off his new ride. Mary needed to run to the store anyway, and John, looking for an excuse to show off his new car, was happy to oblige. So Mary hopped in the front seat. Less than 5 miles from her house, while going around a curve too fast, John lost control of the car and ran into a telephone pole.

John was pronounced dead at the scene. Mary was taken by ambulance to the emergency room where she was shortly pronounced dead. In just 10 minutes, three children lost their mother, and a husband lost his wife.

The subsequent police investigation discovered that John had been drinking alcohol earlier that day, and he was over the legal limit at the time of the accident. All evidence showed that Mary was unaware of John's condition when she got into John's car.

After the customary grieving, the dust eventually settled. The hospital, doctors and ambulance service still wanted payment for services rendered to the tune of just under $100,000. They all placed liens against Mary's estate. In addition, Mary obviously would no longer be able to take care of her family, be a companion to her husband, or contribute financially to the family.

John only had the state's minimum amount of liability insurance, which in Virginia is $25,000 per person. A search was conducted, and it was determined that John had no assets—very little money in the bank, no real estate in his name, no private property to speak of.

Since Mary had just started her new job she wasn't eligible for health insurance yet. She used mass transportation, so she had no car insurance of her own. Therefore, she didn't have any source to pay medical bills and no uninsured motorist coverage.

Mary's husband and their three children came to our office for help.

They wondered how were they going to make it without Mary?

We investigated the accident and discovered all of the above facts. Later we filed a wrongful death claim on behalf of Mary's estate. After an exhaustive search the only insurance available was the $25,000 car insurance coverage. That amount was split between the family and the medical providers. What about the funeral and burial expenses, loss of Mary's future income, Mark's loss of consortium with his wife, the family's mental distress? What about John driving while intoxicated? These were all questions we answered for the family.

Mary's family wanted nothing more than to have their wife and mother returned to them. But that was impossible. And $25,000 wasn't enough to begin to cover Mary's lifetime contribution to household expenses, college tuition for her three kids, or to help her husband pay off their mortgage.

We must ask ourselves the hard questions when looking at our future. If a tragedy occurred today, is your family protected? How can you be sure that your family is appropriately insured? Below are the answers to six frequently asked questions that will help you learn how to protect and defend your family's assets.

6 QUESTIONS EVERY FAMILY MUST ASK TO SEE IF THEY ARE PROTECTED

1. What type of insurance will protect myself and my family?
Insurance primarily protects your family in two situations: 1) if something happens to you, and 2) if you cause harm to someone else. No one expects bad things to happen to them, and only rarely does someone intentionally injure another person. But if you love your family, it's important to be prepared for *anything*. I would never place an infant in a car seat that's not safely buckled in because of what *could* happen. Insurance is no different. It provides peace of mind in the case of a tragedy, which we pray will never occur.

Most families would benefit from considering homeowner's or renter's insurance, auto insurance, umbrella liability insurance, long-term care, life insurance and disability insurance. If you live in a high-risk zone, consider earthquake, wind and rain (e.g., hurricane) and flood insurance.

If you're a business owner, consider including liability, property, "key man" insurance, business interruption, malpractice, life, workers' compensation, and business catastrophic coverage. Discuss all the pros and cons of these with an insurance professional you trust.

2. *How much insurance do I need?*

It depends on what type of insurance, but the overarching rule remains the same. Every family needs enough insurance to *protect their assets*. For example, if you have $100,000 in assets, you need at least $100,000 in insurance coverage to protect those assets. You need insurance to protect your assets and replace your income if you fall victim to a serious accident.

Typically, in the event of accident or injury, you'll need enough coverage to pay all your medical bills and replace all your wages if you miss time from work. If you or a family member causes harm to another, it's imperative you have enough coverage to protect your family's assets if a lawsuit is filed against you. Also, an insurance policy often covers the cost of an attorney to defend you if someone blames you for something that isn't your fault. Therefore, asset protection requires at least more liability insurance than if you've acquired assets.

Take a moment to consider the unthinkable—what if you suffered a serious or fatal injury or illness? Close your eyes and imagine the effect that would that have on your family. To protect your family, consider insurance coverage that pays benefits for those instances, such as life insurance (whole and/or life), health insurance and disability insurance. Statistically, you're much more likely to be disabled than killed.

3. *If someone else causes an accident, won't his or her insurance pay my medical bills and the cost of repairing my car?*

On an average, there are more than 6 million auto accidents per year. More than 3 million people are injured and more than 2 million of those injuries are permanent. In an ideal world, the driver that caused the accident would repair your car and pay your medical bills. But in reality that just isn't the way these things normally play out.

150

First, you must prove the other driver was at fault, which is often not as simple as you may think. After crossing that bridge, the at-fault driver's insurance company won't pay your medical bills as they accrue. They'll make a one-time settlement after you've completed all your medical treatment. In the meantime, doctors and hospitals want to be paid. Mounting medical bills can ruin your credit. Medical bills are one of the top reasons given by families who file bankruptcy.

In addition, figures show that as much as 25 percent of all drivers on the roads are without any car insurance. Of those that do have insurance, many don't have enough car insurance to pay for the damage they cause. Think of Mary's story: *You can't depend on a bad driver to have good insurance.* In some states, such as Virginia, drivers aren't even required to carry liability insurance! So what if they cause an accident and you end up with $100,000 in medical bills. That becomes the concern of you and your family.

You should be realistic in these situations: You could sue the driver at-fault for the accident, but if the driver couldn't afford proper insurance, how likely is he to pay a judgment against him out of his bank account? The driver normally doesn't have insurance because he has no assets to protect. That's why you need to protect yourself and your family.

4. How do I protect myself from uninsured drivers?

It's to your benefit to purchase both *under*insured motorist coverage and *un*insured motorist coverage. You and your family members are the beneficiary of this insurance, meaning that the insurance you purchase is to pay for your own losses, not someone else's.

If you're hurt and the person who was negligent and hurt you doesn't have the appropriate insurance, your own insurance steps in and takes the place of the at-fault driver's insurance. You file a claim to pay your hospital and other medical bills, any wages lost from missing work, and it pays for any property damage such as to have your car fixed.

- Uninsured motorist coverage pays for your losses (and your passengers') if the at-fault driver and owner of the vehicle has no auto insurance.

- Underinsured motorist coverage pays for your losses (and your passengers') if the at-fault driver and owner of the vehicle has too little auto insurance. *The driver that caused the accident that killed Mary was underinsured. Mary's losses greatly exceeded the amount of insurance coverage.*

Mary's story is tragic, but even if you're in a less serious accident, you may have significant medical bills and property damage, and you may miss work. I routinely see emergency rooms bills that involve a CT scan exceed $10,000 and more. That's just for the emergency room bill. Both uninsured and underinsured are relatively inexpensive insurances, and you need them because car accidents are one of the most common ways the average American will get seriously injured.

5. *Why would I need umbrella liability coverage? I don't even know what that is.*

Umbrella liability coverage is also called "personal catastrophic insurance." It's insurance that "sits on top" of your homeowner's, renter's and auto insurance policies. An umbrella policy raises your insurance coverage to the purchased amount; for example $1 million, $3 million, $5 million, or whatever amount is appropriate for you.

You must have strong underlying insurance (home/renter's and auto) before you can purchase umbrella liability insurance, but it's likely the best insurance investment available. Typically, a $1 million umbrella liability policy can be purchased for under $200 per year, and you normally get discounts if you have homeowner's or renter's insurance with the same company as your auto insurance.

An umbrella liability policy protects you and your family's assets in the unlikely event that you cause a catastrophic injury to someone. Again, this is never on purpose or planned. It happens in freak situations. While driving your teenage driver looks down to turn the station and a pedestrian is crossing the street. Or you've been driving all day, and 30 miles from your destination you dose off behind the wheel. Remember, the person that causes the accident is responsible for the damages they cause. If the driver has no assets, there's nothing to fear. But if the driver has equity in a home, savings accounts, a brokerage account, and an account for their kid's college savings, then there's a huge problem. Without an umbrella policy in these instances, you're likely not properly protected. If you cause a horrific car accident or something of the like, this insurance will protect your home, car, investments, bank accounts and other assets.

6. *What does my homeowner's insurance cover?*

Most people are surprised at how broad the typical homeowner's insurance policy is in protecting you and your family's assets. It normally includes fire insurance, which will replace your home, outbuildings and it's contents if your home burns down. It also covers water damage from a leaky pipe or shower. In addition, homeowner's insurance pays for replacement living expenses for a certain time period that you can't live in your home due to damage.

Your homeowner's insurance also protects your assets by paying if your dog bites someone, a person slips and falls on your property, or a temporary worker, such as a roofer or plumber, is hurt on the job. In Virginia, homeowner's policies have also covered accidents that occurred while a family was babysitting a child.

Also, most people think homeowner's policies only cover acts at the home. You have to look at each policy individually, but, for instance, here in Virginia, I've seen several instances where the homeowner's policy protected family members when they committed negligent acts away from home. In one instance, a teenager thought it would be funny to put his friend in a dangerous situation when they were at the park; the kid fell and seriously hurt himself. The homeowner's insurance policy provided liability coverage to help resolve the case brought by the seriously injured friend.

START A CONVERSATION

This chapter is meant to spark a dialogue among families. Laws differ in every state, and they change over time. So you must defer to what's current in your particular state. But, hopefully, this chapter has opened your eyes to re-examine your family's insurance coverage as part of your overall financial plan. My hope is that after reading this chapter you will pull out your insurance policies, mortgages and titles; calculate your assets; and analyze your insurance coverage. Then be honest with yourself: Are you insured adequately to protect you and your family in case of a serious injury to yourself, or if you were sued by someone else? If not, immediately make the necessary changes. Best of luck to you in protecting what you've worked so hard to achieve!

About Damon

Damon Pendleton is an attorney in Virginia at Christina Pendleton & Associates. He concentrates his injury practice around helping families who have lost loved ones as a result of the negligence of others and individuals who have suffered catastrophic injuries at the hands of another person or company.

Prior to attending law school, Damon handled hundreds of cases for one of the largest insurance companies in America. Eventually, Damon became leery of his work with the insurance company after seeing too many injured victims who didn't have competent legal representation against the virtually unlimited resources of insurance companies. Damon switched sides and now, as an insurance company insider, he fights his old bosses over the rights of consumers. Damon provides free information and a list of resources to anyone involved in an accident at www.VirginiasInjuryLawyers.com. Also, at the website under "Free Information" readers can download an "Insurance Policy Checklist" that accompanies this chapter.

Damon's mantra is steeped in age old wisdom: "An ounce of prevention is worth a pound of cure." He looks forward to the time his services are no longer needed. Until that time, his mission is to share ideas with parents on living happy, worry-free lives through instruction on tips to avoid serious injury. He encourages all readers to preorder from his website a free advanced copy of his next book: *Consumer's Guide to Safety for the Family.*

CHAPTER 18

Be Prepared: The 5 Things You Must Know to Get Social Security Disability Benefits

By Debra Shifrin

Most people know someone who's been unable to work for at least a year due to an illness or injury. One of my first Social Security disability clients was a young man in his 30s, who developed a heart condition as a result of a virus. He was a young man with a college degree, who had worked for 10 years in a factory in Barberton, Ohio. One day he started feeling tired and was running a fever. This went on for a while, but he continued to go to work. After a few months of fatigue and fever, he finally went to his doctor. After numerous tests, he was diagnosed with endocarditis (an infection in the heart). The damage caused by the infection resulted in congestive heart failure, and he was placed on a list for a heart transplant.

He was told by his doctor that he couldn't work. Not only could he not work, but he was also told that he needed a new heart and that he may not have long to live. He followed his doctor's advice and applied for Social Security disability insurance benefits. He application was denied, so he filed an appeal. After filing the appeal, he contacted me to represent him on his claim. After being denied for a second time, I requested a hearing on his behalf. Almost three years later, he got a hearing before an Administrative Law Judge and was awarded benefits.

These benefits were crucial because he had to deplete all his savings, risk foreclosure on his house, and borrow money from family and friends. With the benefits, he got a lump sum to pay back the monies he borrowed, a monthly check for current expenses, and most important, Medicare insurance.

The good news is that after finally receiving benefits and knowing that he had monthly income and health insurance, his heart improved sufficiently, to the point that he didn't need a transplant. Relief from stress was a major factor in improving his life.

You may be thinking, "How does this apply to me?" But this can happen to anyone at any time. You need to be prepared and know the five key elements to obtaining Social Security Disability Insurance Benefits.

KEY ELEMENT #1:
UNDERSTAND THE PROGRAMS

There are three major programs within the Social Security Administration: retirement benefits, Social Security Disability Insurance Benefits, and Supplemental Security Income benefits.

As long as you pay FICA taxes, either through your paycheck or self-employment taxes, you're paying for retirement, life insurance and long-term disability policies.

When you reach retirement age, or choose a reduced benefit at age 62, you'll receive your retirement benefits. The amount will be based on the monies you've paid into the system while working.

When you die, your surviving spouse may be able to receive full benefits based on your account. Reduced widow or widower benefits can be received at age 60, or age 50 if the person is disabled. Your spouse will also receive monies until your youngest child is 16 years old or disabled. Your minor children (under age 18 or 19 and still in high school) can also receive benefits. Also, a disabled child can receive benefits as long as they can prove he or she became disabled before age 22. In addition, if you have dependent parents, they can receive benefits if they're over 62 years of age.

You and your family can also receive benefits if you become disabled. As long as you have worked five of the last 10 years and paid into the Social Security system, you may be eligible for Social Security Disability Insurance benefits (DIB). Social Security defines disability as being unable to perform substantial gainful work activity due to a medical condition(s), which will last at least 12 months or will result in death.

If you haven't worked five of the last 10 years, or if your monthly benefit would be less than $698 in 2012, you may be eligible for Supplemental Security Income benefits (SSI). To be eligible for SSI benefits, however, a person must not only be medically disabled but also meet certain financial limitations.

KEY ELEMENT #2:
PROVE YOU'RE DISABLED UNDER
THE SEQUENTIAL EVALUATION

You've worked and paid your FICA taxes for five of the last 10 years, or you financially qualify for SSI. You now have a medical condition or injury that prevents you from working for at least the next year. You think you should be able to receive the monies you've paid into the system. But the government says it's not that clear cut. First, you must go through the sequential evaluation.

The first question is whether you're currently working? None of your medical problems will be considered or evaluated if you're currently able to work. This seems clear cut, but it's the government, and there are always exceptions to every rule. The Social Security Administration defines work as grossing (before taxes and any deductions) less than $1,010 per month. If you earn less than that amount, you won't be considered as working.

Assuming you're not working, the second question is whether you have a severe impairment? A severe impairment is any medical condition or injury that causes limitations and/or restrictions in functioning. This means it must have some affect on your ability to perform your usual work activities.

The third question is whether the disability meets or equals the "Listing of Impairments"? The Social Security Administration has a list of ill-nesses or injuries that are disabling. For you to meet or equal a Listing, you must satisfy every element of the Listing. For example, if you have had reconstructive surgery on a major weight-bearing joint, such as a knee, you would look at Listing 1.03. This Listing requires that you've had the surgery and still cannot ambulate effectively, and you won't be able to ambulate effectively within 12 months of the onset. "Ambulate effectively" is defined as sustaining a reasonable walking pace over a sufficient distance and without companion assistance. Social Security has further defined this as needing a walker, two crutches or two canes. As you can see, it's not easy to meet or equal a Listing.

The fourth question is whether you can return to any of your past rel-evant work? Social Security only considers the work you've done in the past 15 years to be past relevant work. It doesn't matter whether the job still exists. The only question is whether your illness or injury precludes you from performing these jobs.

If you can't perform your past relevant work, the fifth and final ques-tion is whether any jobs exist that a person with your limitations can perform? If there are jobs that a person with your limitations can per-form, you won't be found disabled. If there are no jobs, you'll be found disabled.

KEY ELEMENT #3:
KNOW THE PROCESS

Now you understand how you have to prove disability, but what is the process?

The first thing you have to do is file an application. Social Security has joined the digital age, and applications are usually filed over the internet. The date of your application is important as DIB benefits can only be paid for 12 months prior to the date of your application. Even if you became disabled several years ago, you can only receive monies for the past year. This is also important as you're not eligible for Medicare until you've been able to receive DIB benefits for 24 months. You also need to know that there's a five-month waiting period for DIB. For example, if you're found to be disabled as of January 1, 2010, your benefits will begin June 2010, and you'll be eligible for Medicare June 2012. SSI benefits can only be paid as of the month following the date of your application.

You can either go online yourself, or you can contact a representative to help you file the application. Once you apply, the application is sent to your state Bureau of Disability Determination (BDD) for collection of medical evidence and a decision as to whether or not you're disabled. If you're found to be disabled, you'll receive a Notice of Award, and benefits will begin. If not, in most states you file a Request for Reconsideration. Once again, your file is sent to BDD for a second evaluation. If you're denied again, or if your state doesn't include the reconsideration stage, you have to Request a Hearing. These two steps can take up to a year to complete.

When you Request a Hearing, your file is transferred to your local Office of Disability Adjudication and Review (ODAR). After approximately a year, your case will be set for a hearing before an independent Administrative Law Judge (ALJ). The ALJ will review your file and allow you to appear and testify at a hearing. If the ALJ finds you disabled, you'll be eligible for benefits. If not, you can either file a Request for Review with the Appeals Council or file a new application. If the Appeals Council denies your claim, you have to file a complaint in the appropriate U.S. District Court against the Social Security Administration.

KEY ELEMENT #4:
PROVIDE MEDICAL EVIDENCE

Now you understand the different benefits, know the process to prove you're disabled, and understand the application and appeals processes. One crucial element of the prior three is you must present medical evidence showing that you have an illness or injury that precludes your ability to work.

You need to be seeing a doctor, or other medical professional, on a regular basis. When your file is evaluated, the medical evidence that's supplied by your doctors is reviewed. To prove you have a "severe impairment," which either meets or equals the Listings or precludes you from working, you have to provide medical evidence. One of the most important things for you to remember from this chapter is that if you believe you're disabled, you must provide medical evidence demonstrating the problems that you claim preclude you from working.

Medical evidence is defined by Social Security as documents from licensed physicians, psychologists, optometrists and podiatrists. This includes hospital, doctor and counseling visits, and test results. It's very important that you keep a list of all your doctor and hospital visits, hospitalizations and prescriptions. The documentation of your medical treatment and tests will provide the objective evidence for proving that you're disabled.

KEY ELEMENT #5:
DON'T DO THIS ALONE

Now that I've confused you about the process, I can state that the most important thing for you to remember is that you shouldn't go through this process alone. You need to find an attorney who's familiar with the disability process and can help you navigate the system.

Run the opposite direction if you contact an attorney who says they want a retainer. Attorney fees have been statutorily set at 25 percent of your past-due benefits or $6,000, whichever is less. This means if you receive no past-due benefits, there should be no fee. If your past-due benefits are $10,000, the attorney fees will be $2,500. If your past-due benefits are $60,000, the attorney fees will be $6,000.

You also need to ask any attorney you contact about the number of continuing legal education classes they attend each year to update themselves regarding Social Security. You also should ask how many Social Security hearings the attorney attends each month. The answers to these questions will tell you whether or not you've contacted a knowledgeable attorney who can help you navigate the system and advocate on your behalf.

Just like the person described at the beginning of the chapter, you can never tell when you may be unable to work due to an illness or injury. You need to be prepared to protect and defend your family.

About Debra Shifrin

Debra Shifrin is attorney from Akron, Ohio, who limits her practice to representing the disabled before the Social Security and Veterans' Administrations. Debra is a principal in the firm of Shifrin Newman Smith Inc., a law firm with offices in Akron, Cleveland and Toledo, Ohio.

Debra is a graduate of American University and Case Western Reserve University School of Law. In addition to being admitted to practice law before the Supreme Court of the State of Ohio, Debra is admitted federally to the U.S. District Court for the Northern District of Ohio, the Sixth Circuit Court of Appeals, the Court of Appeals for Veterans Claims, and the U.S. Supreme Court. Debra is also involved in many legal and charitable organizations and is co-recipient, with Dianne Newman, of the Ohio Legal Aid Association Fund's Pro Bono Award in 1999. Debra is currently President Elect of the National Organization of Social Security Claimants' Representatives (NOSSCR) Board of Directors.

Debra enjoys speaking to groups, educating them about the Social Security Administration, being a paperless office and law firm management.

To learn more about Debra, visit her website, www.shifrin-newman.com, call her at (877) 230-5500, or follow her on Facebook or Twitter.

CHAPTER 19

How Much Money Are You *Really* Getting From Your Personal Injury Settlement?

By Don Lowry

Suppose you're a guy or gal who got rear-ended a couple of years ago with the result that you were in the hospital for a couple of days and ended up out of work for a few weeks. After some more tests at the hospital, visits to your family doctor, and six weeks of physical therapy and continuing treatment by a chiropractor, you're feeling pretty good. Your lawyer is ready to settle with the insurance company for the driver who hit you. The policy limit is $50,000, so that's what you agree to settle for, though you might have got more if the policy limit was higher. Fifty thousand dollars sounds pretty good, *but not so fast!*

The lawyer's fee is going to be one-third, or $16,667, and your health insurance company is going to want to recover the $23,500 that they paid for your medical bills so that's going to leave you with only $9,833, a lot less than you had hoped for and not much more than you lost in wages when you were out of work, not to mention that your injury has prevented you from doing the things you like to do like skiing and playing golf.

News reports always tell what big awards accident victims are getting at trial or in settlement, but they leave out what really matters: *how much the client actually receives!*

Some of a lawyer's most important work takes place after the amount of the recovery has been established, and, sad to say, it's work that's sorely neglected by many firms, which means less money and often a lot less for the client. Too many lawyers feel their work is done when the settlement is agreed upon.

Depending on the type of health insurance that paid your medical bills, the $9,833 that you're getting can, in most cases, be easily increased to $17,667 or more, if the lawyer is willing to do the work necessary to get it.

In this chapter, I'll discuss the charges a client faces when settling a personal injury case and ways in which a concerned and caring lawyer can effect reductions, which result in direct savings for the client.

POSSIBLE CHARGES AGAINST THE SETTLEMENT AMOUNT

In every personal injury claim case, there will always be medical bills and often other charges to be dealt with out of the settlement (I'll refer to the amount recovered as the "settlement," even though it may be determined as the result of a trial rather than an agreed amount).

All these become debts owed by the injured person. If they're not paid by insurance or out of the settlement, they'll continue to be owed, and the client may be compelled to pay them later. For example, the doctor's bill will have to be paid by the client if not covered by insurance. Often the client will be unable to pay the doctor bills at the time of receiving the doctor's care, so the bill will still be owed at the time of the settlement.

In addition to doctors' fees, there are many other bills that usually are incurred during the course of the client's recovery from the injury. These include hospital bills, chiropractors, physical therapy, acupuncturist, pain clinics, etc. These are frequently paid by insurance or by government health care programs, such as Medicare and Medicaid (called MaineCare in Maine). The client's own auto policy often will cover some of the medical bills under the medical payments provision (med pay), but most of these sources for getting the bills paid will have to be paid back out of any settlement.

In your situation, you have hospital, physical therapy and chiropractor bills, and we have assumed that all of them were paid by your health insurance.

SOURCES FOR PAYING THE BILLS

Health insurance is, of course, the most common way that medical bills get paid, but health insurance comes in many forms, which determines if, and how much, of the amount paid will have to be paid back when the settlement is received.

Some health insurance plans don't require any repayment of the amounts paid by the insurance company, but most provide for subrogation and some are ERISA (Employment Retirement Income Security Act) plans. When a company is "subrogated" to the claim of the client, it stands in the shoes of the client to recover for the medical bills it paid. ERISA plans are established in connection with an employer's pension plan and are protected by special federal law provisions.

Medical bills may be paid from a number of other sources, in addition to private health insurance. These include the PIP (Personal Injury Protection) provision of the client's policy in no-fault states, med pay (mentioned above), Medicare and Medicaid, workers' compensation, disability insurance, Social Security Disability, and, of course, by the client's out-of-pocket funds. *The rules for paying out of the settlement for each of these sources are all different, so an attorney who has a thorough knowledge of how these all work is able to save bottom-line money for the client.* Let's go over one source at a time and show how a qualified attorney can reduce the pay-back to save money for the client.

PRIVATE HEALTH INSURANCE

As a general rule, the amount to be recovered by a health insurance company from the settlement should be reduced by the cost of collecting the money from the person who caused the injury; in other words, from the settlement. This collection "cost" is the portion of the attorney's fee related to getting back the money for the medical bills, because without the efforts of the attorney, there would be no recovery at all.

In the example where your health insurance company paid $23,500 in medical bills on your behalf, reducing the amount to be paid back to the company by one-third, which covers the attorney's fee, results in lowering the amount to be paid back by $7,833. That's money that goes directly into your pocket!

There are other reasons why the amount to be paid back to the health insurer should be reduced. If the client is forced to accept less than the full value of his or her claim simply because of a low policy limit in the responsible person's insurance, then just as the client isn't being fully compensated, so also should the health insurer have to take a reduction. The same applies when the amount of the client's recovery is compromised because of a dispute about who's responsible for the collision.

The driver who hit you had only a $50,000 policy, but your case may well have been worth more, say $65,000 or $70,000. With this in mind, the lawyer could go to the insurance company and argue that the amount to be paid back should be further reduced because if you're getting less than the full value of your claim, and part of your claim is recovery of medical bills, then you should have to pay back only the reduced amount, which is in the settlement. In your case your lawyer could take the position that you should pay back only 71 percent of the amount the company paid for medical bills, since $50,000 is 71 percent of $70,000. This could mean an additional $4,543 for you. The amount you're going to receive has increased from $9,833 to $22,210!

Another way in which the repayment to the insurance company might be reduced is where there was some dispute as to who was at fault in the accident resulting in a lower settlement because of compromise. Settlement for less than the full value of the case provides another reason why the health insurer shouldn't get repaid in full.

Health insurance companies frequently don't agree that these reductions should apply and will argue that the value of the client's case is less than claimed. Since the value of an injury claim can't be determined with mathematical precision, there's always room for disagreement on how much of a reduction the settlement represents. It's here that the determined attorney will present forceful arguments and where substantial savings can be realized for the client.

ERISA PLANS

If your health insurance is from an ERISA plan, you may not be so lucky. Federal law provides that state laws relating to subrogation or the reduction of liens don't apply, so for these plans, in the absence of some provision in the policy, a full repayment of the amount paid by the health insurance plan may be required with no reduction for costs of collection (attorneys' fees) or for a settlement lower than full value because of a policy limit or contested liability.

ERISA plans, however, come in a wide variety of forms. Some provide for a reduction in the amount to be recovered and some even provide for no pay-back at all. For this reason, it's very important in ERISA cases to carefully examine the provisions of the pension plan under which the policy is written. It's not unusual for an ERISA plan to claim that no reductions will be allowed, when, in fact, a careful examination of the documents will reveal that a substantial savings can be realized for the client.

MED PAY

Med pay, as I mentioned above, is provided under a provision in the client's own automobile policy and is paid to cover medical expenses for the accident-caused injury up to a policy limit. The amount of this coverage is often only $2,000 or $5,000 but may be $10,000 or more. A provision in the auto policy requires that whatever is paid in med pay must be repaid out of the settlement, but the law in many states, including Maine where I practice, requires reduction in the pay-back to account for attorney's fees. Since the usual attorney's fee in a personal injury case is one-third of the settlement, only two-thirds of the amount paid for med pay has to be refunded. Another Maine law provides that if the amount of the settlement is $20,000 or less, then there's no subrogation for any med pay payments (no pay-back).

PERSONAL INJURY PROTECTION (PIP)

Many states have what's known as "no fault" auto insurance, which generally includes what's known as PIP coverage. This covers medical bills, lost wages and funeral expenses, and will be paid regardless of who's at fault in a motor vehicle collision. As with med pay, the insurance company is entitled to subrogation for PIP where there's recovery from a third party.

MEDICAID

Medicaid (called MaineCare in Maine and by different names in several other states) is a health insurance program run by the state, even though it's funded in large part by the federal government. In Maine, as in most states, repayment for medical bills paid by Medicaid are subject to reduction to account for cost of recovery and exigencies of trial, but this still leaves a great deal of room for negotiating where the client's recovery is limited either by a low policy limit or by questionable liability.

WORKERS' COMPENSATION

Many times an injury will occur to a person who's at work, with the result that the employer's workers' compensation insurance company will pay for medical bills as well as an amount to compensate for lost earnings. Although the law protects the employer from any action to recover damages beyond what's paid under workers' compensation, a claim may be made against a third party that caused the injury. Such a claim might include items not paid by workers' compensation, such as pain and suffering and the full value of lost wages.

When a recovery is received from a third party in a workers' compensation case, the workers' comp insurance company is entitled to recover what it has paid to the injured worker and to health care providers, but the rules for the pay-back vary from state to state, so it's important for the lawyer to be familiar with local law.

MEDICARE

Medicare is a federal program to pay for medical care for elderly and disabled people. Federal law provides that the government is entitled to be reimbursed for medical costs related to an injury when there's recovery from a third party. The law also provides for reduction of the amount to be repaid to Medicare by a formula, but the application is very complex and requires knowledge of the laws and rules, plus experience. A mistake in making the Medicare reimbursement can endanger future Medicare coverage for the client and may even result in a later claim for the client to pay back money to the government.

Most Medicare clients have ongoing medical care requirements, which have nothing to do with the injury for which the client is being compensated. Sorting out which payments by Medicare are related to the accident, and thus subject to the reimbursement, and which aren't is an arduous task that requires persistence and patience, because dealing with the Medicare bureaucracy is always difficult.

The laws and regulations on Medicare reimbursement have changed several times in recent years and continue to change, making it necessary for the careful lawyer to constantly re-examine current developments.

OTHER CONSIDERATIONS

Whenever there are claims against the client, there's an opportunity for the lawyer to step in to protect the client's interests and, in most cases, to increase the client's net recovery. Doctors and chiropractors, for example, often bill patients for the full amount but have to reduce fees that are paid by insurance. This provides a good opportunity for the lawyer to negotiate a reduction in a medical bill which is the client's personal responsibility.

Before you're asked to agree to a settlement, the careful lawyer should know enough about the bills and the prospects of getting reductions to give you a fairly accurate picture of what you'll net if the settlement offer is accepted. There should be no surprises.

To sum it up, a lawyer who's willing to put in the extra work can make a big difference in what an injury client receives. The amount of the settlement may sound terrific, but it's what ends up in the client's pocket that really matters.

About Don

Don Lowry is a prominent member of the Maine trial bar who has been engaged in the practice of law for more than 45 years. Following graduation from Brown University, Don served in the Navy as a destroyer and submarine officer before attending Harvard Law School.

In the early '80s, Don started a new firm, Lowry & Associates, concentrating in helping people who've been injured in accidents, and this firm continues with the same goal today.

Don is a member of the American Bar Association, the Maine State Bar Association, the Cumberland Bar Association, the American Association for Justice, and the Maine Trial Lawyers Association. He acts as a volunteer in Cumberland County District Court in representing victims of domestic violence.

Don and Betsy have been married for more than 34 years and have 10 children and 19 grandchildren.

CHAPTER 20

Protect and Defend Your Right to Veterans Benefits

By Francis Jackson

In this chapter, you'll learn how to protect and defend a veteran's right to service-connected compensation for disabling conditions that either began during military service or were caused by military service.[1] Compensation is determined by the Department of Veterans Affairs (VA) based on the type of injury or illness involved. Disabilities are rated on a percentage system by the VA.[2] Depending on the severity of the problem, the VA may rate the condition from zero up to 100 percent disabling; a veteran can have multiple conditions with various ratings.[3]

A TALE OF TWO VETERANS

James and Robert are both Vietnam-era veterans with service in the early to mid-1960s. Both James and Robert receive 100 percent service-connected benefits. First, let's examine James' story.

---

1 Military service, as used in this chapter, means active-duty military service. Certain other kinds of service, such as training for reserves, for example, may not qualify.

2 The VA also has a separate system, called non-service-connected pension. That system is used to compensate veterans who served in various periods of war and who are now disabled but whose disabilities aren't related to their service. This benefit is for low-income veterans and their spouses.

3 The VA doesn't simply add up the various ratings to arrive at the total percentage rating. Instead, it uses a "combined ratings" formula so the final rating for multiple impairments will usually be less than if the various percentages were simply added together. There are also special ratings, such special monthly compensation, available to veterans whose combined ratings may exceed 100 percent.

Veteran James

James applied for benefits in 1995. He explained that he had a nervous condition that dated back to his service. His claim was denied by the VA regional office where he lives in 1996. James then took the first critically important step to protect and defend his right to benefits. He appealed to the Board of Veterans Appeals. Because the law at that time didn't allow James to pay an attorney to represent him, he relied on a non-attorney veterans' service officer. James had an informal presentation before the Board. The judge who heard the case concluded more information was needed. As a result, in 2000 the judge sent the case back to the regional office for further development. After the regional office worked on the case further, it went back to the Board in January 2003. This time the judge decided that the regional office was correct in denying the claim. James then took two critical steps: He appealed the denial to the Court of Appeals for Veterans Claims.[4] He also took advantage of the law passed by Congress to hire an attorney in June 2003 to handle his case before the Court.[5]

The team at the lawyer's office reviewed his claims file. After review, James' lawyer persuaded the lawyer representing the VA that the Board had made errors in handling James' claim and that the claim should be sent back. The Board, in turn, sent the case back to the regional office.

The lawyer also hired a psychologist to review the medical records and write a report. The report showed that James' problems while in the military were the beginning of his nervous disorder. The regional office also sent James for an evaluation. After receiving both reports, the regional office granted benefits to James, giving him a 30 percent rating for his nervous condition.

His lawyer reviewed the medical report that the VA obtained from the examination they arranged, and the existing evidence in the file. The lawyer then advised James that he should appeal to the Board, this time for a higher rating. James authorized his lawyer to appeal. The case went back to the Board, and James' lawyer represented him at the new

---

4 See Docket No. 03-0719.

5 At that time, the law only allowed a veteran to hire and pay a lawyer to represent him (or her) once the claim had been turned down by both the regional office and the Board of Veteran's Appeals. Congress later amended the law so veterans can now hire and pay an attorney to represent them as soon as their claims have been turned down by the regional office.

hearing. He presented James' testimony and the exhibits on his behalf. The lawyer explained to the judge why James was entitled to a 100 percent rating, not just a 30 percent rating.

After the hearing, the judge decided the regional office was wrong, he ordered them to pay James at the full 100 percent compensation level, all the way back to when he first applied in 1995. As a result, even after his lawyer's fees were paid, James was entitled to more than $200,000 in VA benefits.

Sadly, that wasn't the end of the case. Although the Board decided in January 2008 that James was entitled to payment, the VA failed to process his payment. The lawyer wrote to the regional office several times in 2008, pointing out that the Board had awarded benefits and asking about payment. No response was ever received. As a result, at the end of December, 2008, the lawyer filed a petition for extraordinary relief with the court.[6] Within two weeks after the lawyer filed, the regional office notified James of his award. He was paid in full shortly thereafter.

Here James took both of the two steps critical to winning his case in the shortest amount of time and getting the greatest possible amount of benefits. First, he appealed each time the regional office or the Board denied his claim. Second, he hired a lawyer experienced in handling veterans cases to represent him on a contingent fee basis.[7] As a result, from the time he hired an attorney to represent him in his 2003 appeal, things began to happen on his case. Although he had filed his claim in 1995 and had gotten no benefits up to 2003, his case was remanded by the court in 2003, and he was given an initial award of benefits in 2004. By January 2008, he established that the original 2004 award was at too low a rate and was awarded full (100 percent) benefits. With further work, the VA was forced to pay him in full by January 2009.

Veteran Robert

Now, let's compare James' case to what happened with Robert. Robert first applied for benefits in 1968. His claim was found to be service connected but rated at only zero percent, so he received no money. Robert reapplied for benefits repeatedly with the help of various veterans

---

6 See Docket No. 08-4253.

7 A contingent fee simply means that the lawyer agreed to represent James, and he didn't have to pay the lawyer unless the lawyer won his case and got him benefits. James agreed to pay the lawyer 20 percent of his past-due benefits if the lawyer won his case.

service officers (VSOs).[8] He reported to the VA that he suffered from prostatitis, headaches and a nervous condition (described by the doctors as depression). At one point, a VA physician wrote that these three conditions were interrelated and stemmed from the same cause.

Robert continued to apply and reapply. In 1986, his service-connected prostatitis percentage rating was raised from zero to 20 percent and later to 30 percent. In June 1994, Robert stated that his claim was for depression secondary to his service-connected prostatitis. In May 1996, the regional office granted a 70 percent secondary service connection for Robert's nervous condition and a combined service-connected rating of 80 percent, effective June 1994. He was granted a special increase in his benefits, paying him at the 100 percent rate because his conditions made him unemployable. The regional office found the earliest date they could grant for the claim was 1994 when Robert specifically wrote that his nervous disorder was secondary to his service-connected prostatitis.

In 1998, still without a lawyer, Robert filed a CUE (clear and unmistakable error) claim[9] saying he was entitled to an earlier effective date for his unemployability rating. Robert argued that it was a CUE for the regional office in 1996 to find that no claim for secondary service connection for his psychiatric disorder had been made before June 1994. He urged that his prior claims were sufficient to raise an informal claim for secondary service connection. In April 2000, the Board rejected Robert's CUE claim, saying there "was no undebatable error which would have manifestly changed the outcome at the time it was made."

After that denial, Robert finally took the two critical steps. He appealed his case and hired a lawyer. Robert's lawyer briefed his case before the courts, arguing that the Board had held Robert to an unfair standard, failing to take into account that he filed his papers with the VA as a lay person, not a skilled attorney. The lawyer persuaded the appeals court

---

8 Veteran's service officers are employees of various organizations such as the Paralyzed Veterans of America (PVA), the American Legion, the Order of the Purple Heart, Amvets, Disabled American Veterans (DAV), etc. Veterans service officers are non-lawyers who've been hired by their organization to work with veterans claims. Training varies considerably from one organization to another. Because VSOs are not lawyers, they only handle claims at the VA level, not before the courts.

9 This is the only type of claim allowed by the VA regarding a decision that wasn't appealed in time. CUE stands for clear and unmistakable error. Section 3.105 of Title 38 of the Code of Federal Regulations allows a veteran to file a CUE claim when he believes that a prior decision by the department wasn't merely wrong but so obviously, clearly wrong that a new review will reveal an unmistakable, undebatable error in the prior decision. Unfortunately, this type of claim is extremely difficult to win.

that Robert's claim hadn't been fairly decided, and the case was sent back for further review.[10]

Unfortunately, the VA still didn't grant Robert's claim to an earlier onset date for his benefits, and his lawyer had to appeal again. Once again the case had to be appealed to the Court of Appeals. There Robert's lawyer and the VA lawyers worked out a settlement agreement to review the merits of Robert's claims for an earlier start date for his benefits, and the appeal was dismissed.[11] Following the settlement, the regional office reviewed Robert's claim but again denied it. Robert's lawyer appealed that denial to the Board of Veterans' Appeals. However, the Board refused to review the case based on the terms of the settlement, claiming that later court cases had changed the law and it didn't have to follow the settlement. Once again, Robert's lawyer had to appeal the case to the courts. The Court agreed that the Board was wrong and remanded the case again, ordering the Board to comply with the terms of the settlement.[12] Robert's claim will once again go back to the Board for further proceedings.

DEFENDING YOUR BENEFIT RIGHTS

The events involving James and Robert show there are two equally critical steps in protecting and defending the right to service-connected compensation. If you're a veteran with a disability, which began during service or which is otherwise connected to your service, you start by making a claim to the VA. Some claims are granted by the VA early in the claims process. However, if your claim is partly or totally denied, you must take two critical steps to protect and defend your right to compensation.

The First Critical Step

The first critical step is always to file a timely appeal. To appeal the regional office decision, you file a notice of disagreement (NOD), which is very informal.

The notice must meet three requirements. First, it must be in writing. Second, whatever you submit in writing must specifically say both that you disagree with the decision *and* that you desire to appeal. Third, your written statement or letter must be received by the VA within one year of the date of the cover letter sending you the decision you are appealing.

10 See 360 F.3d 1306 (Fed. Cir. 2004).
11 See 128 Fed.App'x 152 (Fed. Cir. 2005).
12 See the decision in Docket No. 09-4606, November 23, 2011.

Once the VA receives your NOD, they'll issue a Statement of the Case and send you a Form 9. To complete your appeal you must fill out the Form 9 and return it to the VA. There's generally a 60-day deadline from the date of the VA letter sending you the statement of the case. If you file an NOD *and* a Form 9 within the time allowed, you'll have taken the first critical step.

The Second Critical Step

The second critical step to protecting your right to compensation is to find an attorney with experience with veterans' claims. The VA process is full of potential pitfalls. Under the most recent change to the law, veterans can now hire an attorney to represent them with the VA as soon as they have received a decision from the regional office. It will be most useful to hire an attorney as soon as possible after the date of the decision because of the time limits to appeal.

LESSONS LEARNED

For service-connected compensation benefits, you start by making a written application to the VA. If you're not granted all the benefits you asked for, *the first critical step to protect and defend your right is to file an appeal within the time limits.* Because Robert failed to appeal the various VA decisions, it took him from 1968 to 1994 to get to 100 percent benefits with the VA, even though he had been found disabled by Social Security.

The second critical step is to hire a lawyer experienced in veterans' claims as soon as you receive an unfavorable decision. James did that and resolved his claim. Robert missed the chance to appeal, so his lawyer has had to repeatedly go all the way to the federal courts just to keep his claim for an earlier effective date going. Because Robert failed to hire an attorney and to appeal his effective date in the 1996 decision within the appeal time, his claim for an earlier date has now taken 14 years, and the claim has not yet been won, although the end appears to finally be in sight.

About Francis

Francis "Jack" Jackson is an experienced attorney who specializes in disability law for those seeking veterans disability benefits and Social Security disability benefits. Francis, founding partner of Jackson & MacNichol, Attorneys at Law, has been featured on NBC, CBS, ABC and FOX network affiliates around the country.

Francis most recently appeared as a guest of Ben Glass on the "Consumer Advocate" show discussing his expertise in benefits for veterans and Social Security Disability Benefits and how his practice allows him to make a significant difference in the lives of people facing disabilities. He has also been quoted in *USA Today.*

Looking back on the roots of Francis' more than 30-year career as an attorney, after his graduation summa cum laude from Bowdoin College in 1974, a factor in his move to disability law was his longtime interest in the mental health and law area. That sprang from his internship during law school with the prestigious Mental Health Law Project in Washington, DC. While in law school, he also served on the editorial board of the University of Maine *Law Review* and was a member of the school's national moot court competition team.

Jack has practiced law for more than 30 years, focusing on the disability area. After he established his Social Security disability practice, he expanded the firm's practice areas to include representation of veterans seeking disability benefits. As a member of the National Association of Veterans Advocates (NOVA), Jack's firm, Jackson & MacNichol, represents veterans at all stages of the benefits appeal process and has handled hundreds of cases nationwide. In addition to representing clients before the Veterans Administration, the firm represents veterans in the appeals courts. Among Francis' more important victories in veterans cases at the court level are *Smith v. Derwinski*, 2 Vet. App. 241 (1992) and *Moody v. Principi*, 357 F.3d 1370 (Fed. Cir. 2004).

Jack tracks the latest developments in these practice areas through memberships in organizations such as NOVA. In addition to developing cases through careful investigation, including the review of medical records, interviews and collection of evidence, he and the other lawyers at Jackson & MacNichol are trained litigators, with extensive experience representing clients in hearings and with legal knowledge to write persuasive briefs.

In addition to representing veterans, Francis also helps people obtain the Social Security Disability Benefits that they deserve. While many lawyers who do Social Security disability work are intimidated by the federal courts and shy away from such cases,

Francis and his firm regularly win cases in the courts. Francis has even written a book on the topic: *How Not to Lose Your Social Security Case.* When people retain Jackson & MacNichol, they know they're getting lawyers who aren't afraid to fight for justice for them.

To learn more about Francis Jackson, disability lawyer, visit www.jackson-macnichol. com, see the Jackson & MacNichol Facebook page, or call toll-free (800) 5224-3339.

CHAPTER 21

Arrested for DUI?
Use the *Forgotten* Defense—
No Probable Cause to
Arrest for DUI!

By George F. McCranie IV, Esq.

You probably never thought it would happen to you. As you were driving, you entered a roadblock or a police officer pulled you over and accused you of drunk driving.

You had a couple of drinks but not many. You felt fine to drive home, but why did the officer (single you out and) stop you? Now what? What happens next? How are you going to defend yourself? Will you go to jail? Are you going to be fined and put on probation? Is your picture going to be in the newspaper? Will you lose your job? All these questions are important, and you need answers.

My upcoming book *Down and Dirty DUI Defense* (in Georgia) was written to educate people, who've been accused of DUI or have a friend or family member who is in the same unfortunate position. Being charged with DUI is extremely serious and can have very severe consequences for you, as well as an emotional and financial impact on your family.

Because of the reported rising number of deaths and injuries that have been related to DUI accidents, many states are imposing stiffer penalties on the offenders. In the state of Georgia, where I practice, DUI is considered a criminal offense, and a DUI conviction will remain on your criminal record for the rest of your life.

If you're convicted of a first DUI, you face mandatory jail time, a license suspension, community service, pay for and complete a DUI risk reduction class (DUI School), and be required to serve 12 months on probation. Your automobile insurance premiums could sky rocket, and you can even be disqualified for the remainder of your life when applying for life insurance. As you can see, having an experienced and qualified lawyer who can represent you is a must. This is serious business, and your attorney should know how to challenge the evidence that will be used against you.

Being a State prosecutor and then having represented and defended DUI clients since 1998, I'm uniquely experienced and qualified to educate you on the reasons people are arrested for DUIs. I will give you examples of typical evidence officers use to meet the legal standard of *probable cause* that's necessary to arrest you for DUI. I will enlighten you on some of the tactics you can use to defend yourself, as well as the importance and urgency of hiring a qualified, competent and experienced DUI attorney to represent you.

If you don't remember anything else from this chapter, you need to remember that everything you *say or do will* be used against you by the officer and prosecutor. That means if you tell the officer you've had "just one glass of wine with dinner," or a "couple of beers while watching the game," it will be included in the police officer's incident report. However it won't be reported the way you explained it; most likely the officer will report "driver admits to consuming alcohol." If the officer notices that you have "red and blood shot eyes" and an "odor of an alcoholic beverage on or about your person," I can guarantee you it will be in his report, and the prosecutor will make sure this evidence comes out during trial.

It's important that you understand the reason for the arrest, as well as what to expect should you go to trial and have to defend yourself. When an officer stops a suspected drinking driver, there were clues the officer noticed that aroused suspicion and caused the officer to turn on his emergency lights, single you out and stop you. When that happens, it's important to know *what to do* and *how to handle* yourself in a way that will improve your chance for a successful outcome in this dreaded situation. Many times defense attorneys and their clients place all their eggs in one basket and focus solely on defeating the state's breath, blood or urine test results. However, before the prosecutor gets to the test results he must *first* prove that the officer had *probable cause* to arrest you for DUI.

There are three phases in a DUI stop *before* an arrest. Many states, including Georgia, train their officers using the National Highway Traffic Safety Administration (NHTSA) Standards and Procedures. Each of the phases is discussed in-depth in my upcoming book *Down and Dirty DUI Defense* (in Georgia). During the three phases, the officer may be able to gather all the evidence he needs to convict you of DUI, even without the states breath, blood or urine test results. An effective and aggressive defense based on the officer's lack of *probable cause* to arrest you for DUI is often more effective than simply trying to *suppress* or "keep out" the state's test results.

PHASE 1:
THE OFFICER'S OBSERVATION OF YOUR DRIVING

You need to understand what prompted the officer to pull you over while driving. Just your driving behavior alone can send signals to other drivers, as well as to a police officer, that you could be intoxicated.

There are cues that officers look for prior to activating emergency lights and pulling you over. Some of the cues an officer is taught to look for include:

- Weaving and weaving across lanes. The best example I can give you of this cue is the recent public service commercial showing the truck with its cab filled with beer and the driver all over the road before being stopped at a roadblock.

- Almost striking another object or vehicle.

- Turning with a wide radius. This cue was recently one of the top reasons for stopping a suspected drinking driver in the metro Atlanta area.

- Driving on something other than a designated roadway. In my experience, cases where the driver was in the ditch or driving in the median can be challenging.

- Appearing to be impaired. A recent example of this cue that I was involved with was a driver sitting at a red light and an officer notices that the driver has a cigarette that has burned all the way to the filter and is hanging from the driver's lip. The light turns green, and the driver fails to react for over 10 seconds.

- Straddling the center lane. This is a classic example of bad driving that attracts unwanted attention.

- Driving into opposing or crossing traffic.

- Slow response to traffic signals. Remember the driver with the cigarette!

- Turning abruptly or illegally. This is sometimes used to give the officer *reasonable articulable suspicion* to stop a driver near a roadblock.

There are also cues the officer is looking for after the lights are activated:

- An attempt to flee

- No response to emergency equipment

- An abrupt swerve

- Striking the curb or another object

These are not the complete lists of the cues officers are trained to look for but are some of the most common reasons that initiate a DUI investigation.

You might be surprised to learn that *speeding is not one of the cues that a driver is intoxicated*. However, driving more than 10 mph *under* the posted speed limit is a cue. When you get behind the wheel of your vehicle, pay close attention to your driving. If you're stopped, the officer is going to be watching everything you do and listening to every word you say. Often my clients tell me that the officer said he stopped them for "failure to maintain lane or weaving." Many times a driver has legitimate reasons for the perceived "bad driving," such as adjusting the radio, fumbling with navigation devices, disciplining a child, or even retrieving a dropped cell phone. (Very common in my area for the past five years). If given the opportunity to explain any bad driving, take full benefit of the opportunity to explain the reason you "weaved" or "failed to maintain lane."

Being pulled over for suspicion of bad driving is just the beginning of the officer's observations of you and the end of Phase 1. A good tactic many experienced DUI defense attorneys use on cross examination of the officer is to question him on what cues the driver *didn't* exhibit. If you were stopped for "weaving," look back at the cues I've given you, and you'll see how this tactic can be used effectively. The point is to explain the innocent reason you have for the perceived "bad driving."

PHASE 2:
THE OFFICER'S OBSERVATION AND PERSONAL CONTACT WITH YOU *AFTER* THE STOP

In my years of defending drinking drivers, Phase 2 can often make or break a clients' defense despite being able to explain some bad driving and OK performances on the standardized field sobriety tests (SFSTs). There are 28 cues that officers are looking for, which are taught under the NHTSA training program used in many states.

The 28 cues are broken down into the following categories:

• *Things the officer sees,* such as open container of alcoholic beverage, prescription pill bottles, driver produces the wrong documents, driver fumbles or drops his driver's license, driver leaves the vehicle in gear, and the driver's bloodshot and watery eyes.

• *Things the officer smells,* such as the odor of an alcoholic beverage, distinctive smell of marijuana or "cover-up" odors like breath strips, mouthwashes, or even the unusually strong breath mints that come in a metal tin.

• *Things the officer hears,* such as the driver's admission of drinking or use of prescription or illegal drugs, slurred speech, abusive language and inconsistent responses. If the officer suspects you of DUI, don't expect to simply talk your way out of it. *At my office, my motto is, "Admit Nothing, Deny Everything, Demand Proof*SM. My standard advice is probably the same as your mother has given you, "If you can't say anything good, don't say anything at all!" The best tactic is to politely not answer any questions that can be used against you at trial. If asked: "Have you been drinking tonight?" or "How much have you had to drink?" a wise answer would be: "Officer, if you suspect alcohol, can I call my attorney?" or "Officer, if you suspect alcohol, shouldn't you advise me of my rights?

All the observations the officer makes will be noted in his DUI incident/ arrest report. An aggressive defense based on the officer's training manual and published NHTSA reports can be very effective by showing that NHTSA doesn't include his observations as valid cues for an intoxicated driver. Many officers have a very surprised look on their face in court when asked to read the published NHTSA studies that have specifically *removed* the cues "bloodshot and watery eyes" and "odor of an alcoholic beverage."

PHASE 3:
THE STANDARDIZED FIELD SOBRIETY TEST (SFST)

The field sobriety test includes three separate tests:

- Horizontal Gaze Nystagmus (HGN)
- Walk and Turn
- One Leg Stand

Standardized procedures have been created for administering these tests by NHTSA, and officers usually attend a three-day training program that concludes with the students being required to accurately give instructions for the tests and administer them correctly. I've personally attended a training program administered by former law enforcement, and it's a very detailed and structured training program. For days on end officers are taught DUI detection and general deterrence, how to take investigative notes (even what descriptive terms to use), how to testify in court, how to give the instructions for the SFSTs and how to correctly administer the SFSTs. (For a detailed examination of the NHTSA SFST, get my upcoming book *Down and Dirty DUI Defense*).

The training the officers receive is top notch. However, due to the passage of time, not administering the SFSTs on a daily basis, laziness, or simply wanting to cut corners to save time, officers often get sloppy when giving the instructions for and in the actual administration of these tests. By using the officer's NHTSA student training manual against him I've often been able to demonstrate that the SFSTs instructions were given improperly and/or the actual administration of the SFSTs was significantly flawed. In court, I've seen officers throw up a little in their mouths (just a little) when they testify and give improper instructions or leave out steps in the administration of the SFSTs. Having their *mistakes* brought to light by a defense attorney in open court is an officer's *nightmare!*

When asked to take the SFSTs, is it fair that you as the test subject haven't had an opportunity to practice, probably didn't understand all the instructions (if the officer even gave you the *correct* instructions), and many times weren't given a demonstration of the test by the officer. The field sobriety tests are all *voluntary*. You are under no legal requirement (in Georgia) to perform these tests. By even attempting to perform these tests you can give the officer valuable evidence to use against you in court. My standing advice is **do not take the SFST.** *Remember my motto: "Admit Nothing, Deny Everything, Demand Proof SM."*

After reading all this I bet you would like to learn three little-known *secrets* to prove the officer didn't have *probable cause* to make the arrest for DUI.

- *Secret #1: When given the opportunity to explain any "bad driving," take it.* Explain in a clear and calm manner that you "may have weaved" due to an everyday occurrence such as changing the radio station, working with your GPS, or retrieving a dropped personal item, even a cell phone. A simple explanation for the "bad driving" can resonate with a jury.

- *Secret #2: When the officer talks to you, don't make any statements or respond to any questions where your answers can be used against you in court.* When asked "Have you been drinking," a fair response would be "Officer if you suspect DUI, shouldn't you read me my Miranda rights" or "Can I call my attorney before answering any questions?" Many of my clients will say that if the officer suspects you're under the influence, you're not going to be able to *simply* talk your way out of it.

- *Secret #3: Don't take the SFSTs.* The SFSTs are completely *voluntary*. You're under no obligation to take them. My standing advice to clients (in Georgia) is to *refuse the SFSTs*. Most people can't perform these tests under perfect conditions. Problems such as injuries and medical conditions, age, being overweight, type of footwear, weather conditions, uneven ground, strobe lights and passing traffic are just a few of the reasons drivers "fail" the SFSTs every day. By knowing these *secrets* and following my advice, you can deny the officer and prosecutor important evidence that they would normally use against you in court, and you can protect your right against self-incrimination.

About George

Douglas, Georgia, DUI Lawyer George McCranie has gained fame throughout Georgia for his success in DUI defense. Whether defending professional athletes or college students, his aggressive style of defense has made him the "go to DUI attorney" in his area. He's the author of the upcoming book on DUI in Georgia titled *Down and Dirty DUI Defense*. A former Georgia Assistant District Attorney, George has earned the respect and confidence of his clients through hard work and his aggressive defense. For more information on George, visit www.mccranielawfirm.com or email him at georgemccranie@mccranielawfirm.com.

CHAPTER 22

Are Jacks Wild?
How 1 Night of Fun
Can Ruin a Life

By Jeffrey A. Luhrsen, Esquire

Seventeen-year-old Jack Martin stepped out of the shower and looked in the mirror. His eyes were deep brown and his hair short, almost a crew cut. He wondered when he'd be able to grow a beard like his dad. "Good things come to those who work and wait," his mother liked to say. Jack was OK with working but was sick of waiting. He was already 17 and didn't even have a driver's license, let alone any real plan for a car.

His big sister, Cate, knocked gently on the door of the bathroom they shared. "Aren't you done yet?" she asked. "Piss off, Kick," he said evenly. He had always called her "Kick." He couldn't remember why and didn't care. To him, she was "Kick," and that was that.

He looked into the mirror again. Skinny, he thought. Then he took his towel and wiped some of the steam away. Definitely skinny, he assessed. So he flexed his neck, shoulders, and chest, and showed off his tattoos the way his favorite UFC fighters did. It didn't help.

"Rachel" was in black on his left chest, and "Zoe" was in blue on his right shoulder. He closed his eyes and remembered the smell of their shampoos and the feel of their skin against his. He thought idly about which one he loved more, or hated more, depending on how you looked at it. "Whatever," he thought, reminding himself that they were nothing to him anymore.

He was looking forward to starting a driver's education course after Christmas. He would finish the course and get his license, somehow, some way, over the summer. If he was lucky enough to find a job, he might buy a used car. He was studying auto mechanics at East Bay Tech, and he was a fast learner. He'd need help getting a job from East Bay's principal, Mack Overstreet, and Mr. Overstreet was a well-known tool so that could be a problem. "First things first," he thought.

It was already dark out. He needed to get over to Rip's place. He and Rip were going to play Modern Warfare on Xbox live. Rip's older brother, Marcus, bought the Xbox and the big screen TV a few months before. Marcus always had money but never a job.

Rip wasn't afraid to talk with girls, or even women. Jack was on the quiet side, so hanging out with Rip and Marcus wasn't a bad idea. Marcus and Kick had graduated together. She said he had always been disgusting and that was why he was still chasing high school girls.

Jack cracked the bathroom door and checked the hallway for Kick or her 7-year-old son, Alfonso, who his parents called "The Fonz," for reasons passing understanding. He walked to the room he shared with The Fonz and silently closed the door. Jack surveyed his neatly organized shoe collection. Nike, then Reebok, then Adidas. Reebok, he decided. He threw on some jeans that were loose enough to be cool but not so baggy that they fell into the "butt-crack, idiot, wanna-be gangsta" look forbidden by his dad. Next came a green hoodie with "Hurley" across the chest.

Jack high-fived The Fonz, shouted good-byes to his parents, and headed for the door. Kick looked up from her book, smiled and said, "You have no shot." Jack paused, meeting her eyes, and smiling back casually while he silently showed her the middle finger of his right hand. He heard her laughing as he hopped onto his bicycle.

Marcus was at Backstreet Bar talking with the owner about renting a room for a party. "Two hundred bucks and the room is yours until 2:30, but anybody who wants to come into the bar has to show ID. Oh yeah," the owner continued, "the security deposit is another $200 and you gotta buy the beer from me. Look," Marcus said, "I'll give you $600 for the room and the deposit and 15 cases of beer, as long as you're not gonna bug me about who comes and goes or who drinks and who doesn't." The owner thought it over. "You get 10 cases of beer, and I don't give a damn who you bring or what you do."

Marcus got out his new Droid and texted everybody in his phone book. "Party at Backstreets tonight! Free beer. Make sure the girls from Riverside and West Chase know!" Almost everybody in Marcus's phonebook was still in high school.

It was just past 8 when smart phones all over the Eastside buzzed. Within minutes, news of the Backstreets party went viral. By 9 o'clock, kids started showing up. One of the bouncers made up signs with big arrows so all the kids would know where to go and where to stay.

Mikey Williams was a senior at West Chase. His part-time girlfriend posted a message about the Backstreets party on Facebook. Mikey didn't like the guys from Riverside. He texted his crew: "Meet me at the Wal-Mart parking lot in 30, and we'll go from there. Be ready to rumble."

Hector McGlockton was a senior at Riverside. One of his boys from West Chase called him about the party. "Mikey Williams is going," Hector heard through the cell static. "He's a prick," Hector said. It was settled. Hector and his boys would be there.

Jack and Rip stayed close to the walls in the packed room at Backstreets. Every so often one of the bouncers would come in and shove another 12 pack into a cooler, and somebody would give him a $20 bill. There was a game of quarters at one table, and some guys were having a chugging contest at another. As long as the kids kept the money coming, the bouncers kept the beer coming. It was the natural order of things.

It was almost midnight when Jack pointed to his watch and mouthed, "Gotta roll." Rip put a bottle of Jaeger Meister to his mouth and nodded as he drank. When Jack made it outside, he filled his lungs with a deep breath of cool air that didn't smell of beer and too much cologne. He let it out slowly through his nose and saw his bike in the distance, where nobody would see it, or him, when he left.

Two drunk guys were jawing at each other on the left side of the long, rectangular parking lot. They had their boys behind them, maybe 8 or 10 each. Jack thought some looked like they had stepped out of a J. Crew ad, while others were going for the tough guy look.

Marcus was in a car doing business when he heard the commotion. He recognized that punk Mikey Williams right away. As he walked toward them, he heard somebody say, "Bust him in his eye, Hector!" Mikey had a Budweiser in his right hand, and he pointed his left index finger about an inch from Hector's nose and said something. Hector put his beer down and said, "You're gonna get hurt." Mikey put his drink down, too, and started to circle Hector.

Marcus was almost there when Mikey saw him. "What's up?" Mikey said just before Marcus' right fist slammed into the left side of his jaw. Mikey's knees buckled and Hector stepped forward and stuck a knee into Mikey's navel. Somebody broke a Miller Lite bottle over the back of Marcus's head just as somebody else, probably a wrestler Jack thought, took Hector to the ground. It was chaos.

Jack started running to his right when he saw Marcus drop to his knees. Hector's guys were going after Mikey's boys, but Mikey's crew—they were all over Marcus. Jack was almost there when he heard himself yell, "Cops! The cops are here!" Jack grabbed Marcus and, surprised by his own strength, snatched him to his feet and kept running. Jack was almost to his bike and was thinking about what to do next when he felt like he had been hit in the upper left side of his back by a bowling ball shot out of a cannon. There had been a loud noise, maybe a firecracker. Jack felt another bowling ball hit him, this time in his lower back. He wondered about the firecrackers as he was thrown onto his face.

Jack pulled his knees to chest and noticed that everything was cold, ice cold, except his hands. They were warm and wet. He saw dark blood pouring between his fingers. He wondered, "Is this what they mean on Call of Duty when they say a guy is bleeding out?"

No way," he thought. "It was just firecrackers." Then everything went black.

The first round from the Glock entered his back a few inches below his left shoulder blade. It left an explosive exit wound right where the "c" in

"Rachel" had been. The second round hit him in the center of his back, about 6 inches up from his tailbone. It blew his abdominal aorta in two, just like a rubber tube cut in half with a straight razor. The abdominal aorta is the largest artery in the abdomen, carrying freshly oxygenated blood from the heart. That's why Jack's blood was so dark, almost like a plum. John Michael Martin was dead within 90 seconds of hitting the ground.

The sheriff said the shooter would be prosecuted "to the fullest extent of the law," and she was considering charging Marcus with giving alcohol to minors, a misdemeanor. The owner of Backstreets said, "Backstreets officially condemns underage drinking and had no knowledge that minors were drinking on the premises." The local beer distributors issued a press release expressing sympathy and urging greater "personal responsibility" to avoid such tragedies in the future.

Mr. Overstreet renamed the West Bay Tech auto mechanics shop for Jack, after his parents buried him. With denial and confusion in his green eyes, The Fonz asked his mother, "How could this happen?" Kick met her son's gaze and answered with tears. Just tears.

HOW TO SAVE LIVES

This fictional story was inspired by actual events, but it could happen to anyone's child, and unfortunately, it does all too often. How do we address this problem? The National Institute on Alcohol Abuse and Alcoholism published a paper on underage drinking prevention (http://pubs. niaaa.nih.gov/publications/arh26-1/5-14.htm). In *Strategies to Prevent Underage Drinking*, the authors suggest a multidimensional approach, the highlights of which are discussed below.

School Strategies
School-based programs should reduce the onset and prevalence of adolescent alcohol use by decreasing personal and social risk factors and strengthening personal and social protective factors. The following factors are critical:

- The development of personal, social and resistance skills to help students identify internal pressures (e.g., anxiety and stress) and external pressures (e.g., peer pressure and advertising) to use drugs and to give students the skills to resist these pressures while maintaining friendships

- An emphasis on normative education that reinforces the awareness that most adolescents do not use alcohol, tobacco or other drugs

- Structured, broad-based skills training, such as goal setting, stress management, and communication, general social and assertiveness skills

- Interactive teaching techniques, such as role playing, discussions and small-group activities to promote active student participation

- Multiple sessions over several years, particularly during middle school

- Teacher training and support from program developers or prevention experts

- Active family and community involvement

Family Strategies

Family involvement is important for the success of alcohol prevention strategies. Parent-child relationships, discipline methods, communication, monitoring and supervision, and parental involvement can significantly reduce adolescent alcohol use. Promising family strategies for preventing alcohol, tobacco, and other drug use include structured, home-based parent-child activities; family skills training, behavioral parent training and behavioral family therapy. The following parenting skills are important for the prevention of alcohol use:

- Improving parent-child relations by using positive reinforcement, listening and communication skills, and problem solving

- Providing consistent discipline and rule making

- Monitoring children's activities during adolescence

- Strengthening family bonding

The Preparing for the Drug-Free Years (PDFY) program consists of five competency-training sessions for parents, with young adolescents attending one of those sessions together with their parents. Comparisons with control families found positive effects on parents' child-management practices and parent-child relations, improved youth resistance to peer pressure toward alcohol use, reduced affiliation with antisocial peers, reduced levels of problem behaviors, and delayed substance use initiation.

A less intense family involvement approach is based on including parents in homework assignments around issues of alcohol use, thereby increasing the likelihood that alcohol, tobacco, and other drug use is discussed at home, and potentially enhancing parenting skills by increasing communication between parent and child and providing behavioral tips to parents.

Policies to Reduce Commercial Access

To address the problem of alcohol availability from commercial providers, communities have conducted enforcement campaigns using compliance checks. During these checks, law enforcement officers supervise attempts by kids to purchase alcohol. When an illegal sale is made, penalties are applied to the seller.

Other policy tools to reduce youth access to alcohol from commercial sources include requiring servers of alcohol to be trained to detect false identification. However, studies show that such programs by themselves are unlikely to reduce sales to minors. Some states have enacted Dram Shop laws that allow third parties to sue vendors who sell alcohol to minors when it results in death or injury.

Policies to Reduce Social Access

Policy tools for limiting youth access to alcohol from social providers attempt to reduce the frequencies of underage drinking parties and of adults illegally providing alcohol to kids. Some of these prevention approaches are being implemented at the community level. For example, communities may address underage drinking parties by creating enforcement mechanisms, such as noisy assembly ordinances, that allow law enforcement officers to enter private residences where underage drinking is occurring. (An example can be found at www.epi.umn. edu/alcohol.) Communities can also require beer kegs to be registered at the time of sale. Using a keg's unique identification number, police can identify adult purchasers of kegs used at parties where underage guests drink. To deter adults from illegally giving alcohol to minors, some states have enacted social host laws that allow third parties to sue social providers who give alcohol to minors when it results in death or injury.

About Jeffrey

Jeffrey A. Luhrsen was an honor student at the University of Tampa before studying law at Stetson University and Temple University. He graduated from U.T. in 1990 and from Stetson, with honors, in 1993. He earned an LL.M. in Trial Advocacy from Temple University Beasley College of Law in 2008.

Mr. Luhrsen served as a Judge Advocate in the U.S. Army JAG Corps. As a Judge Advocate, he served as Trial Counsel, Military Magistrate, and Special Assistant U.S. Attorney with the U.S. Department of Justice.

Following his JAG service, Jeff returned to Florida in 1998 and has been representing only consumers with tort claims and insurance disputes ever since. He concentrates on alcohol safety cases, representing DUI victims and victims of underage drinking, including teenagers.

He was chair of MADD Florida's Public Policy Council in 2007 and currently serves as Chair of the Legislative Committee for the Sarasota Coalition on Substance Abuse.

Professional associations and recognitions include the highest possible ratings in legal ability and ethical standards from Martindale-Hubbell and memberships in the Florida Bar, the Virginia Bar, and the Florida Justice Association. He is a Fellow of the Academy of Florida Trial Lawyers and a member of the Multi-Million-Dollar Advocates Forum *(limited to attorneys with multi-million-dollar verdicts or settlements)*. In 2007, the *Bradenton Herald* recognized Luhrsen Law Group as the "Best Law Firm" in Manatee County.

Mr. Luhrsen has been featured in the following publications: *Florida Justice Association Journal*, September 2007: "Legal Grave Robbing: Discovery of Psychotherapy Records in Florida Wrongful Death Cases"; and *Florida Bar Journal*, November 2008: "Back to the Future."

He and his wife, Julie, are both attorneys; they have two children.

CHAPTER 23

Speak Up! Immunity Laws Must be Stopped

By Ben Glass

Why do we allow charities and government employees to get away with causing serious injury to people least able to protect themselves? Consider the following cases:

JUAN JIMENEZ V. DIDLAKE INC.

On April 13, 2007, Iris Figueroa-Jimenez sent her 25-year-old severely disabled son, Juan, off to his adult day-care facility, Didlake, in Prince William County, Virginia. Didlake is a huge organization that provides both rehabilitative care and jobs for the severely disabled. It earns more than $32 million per year in revenue, in large part because it has millions of dollars in government contracts providing workers for various federal agencies.

Though he has been confined to a wheelchair and is severely mentally disabled, virtually uncommunicative, and totally dependent on others since he had a stroke when he was young, Jimenez was otherwise healthy when he went to Didlake that day.

At the end of the day he was transported back home. When he saw his mother he groaned to her that his leg hurt. It turns out that he had a severely fractured leg, one that would require surgery and the implantation of a rod to be repaired.

Iris Figueroa-Jimenez sued Didlake on behalf of her son in the Circuit Court in Prince William Country, Virginia, alleging that employees there had carelessly injured him.

ADIJAT OLA V. YMCA

In April 2002, Adijat Ola, then 13, was abducted and sexually assaulted in a bathroom of the YMCA in Hampton Roads, Virginia. She suffered major injuries because of the assault. She and her family were members of the YMCA and paid a fee to use the swimming pool that day.

Her parents sued the YMCA, alleging that it had been negligent in allowing the perpetrator, a non-member, to use the facility and then in failing to repair a lock on the bathroom door. They claimed that the assault and injuries to their daughter were preventable with reasonable care.

ALI HILAL V. THE CITY OF ALEXANDRIA SCHOOL BOARD

On October 16, 2009, Hayat Ramadan, greeted her 8 year old son, Ali, as he came home from his Alexandria, Virginia, elementary school. Ali, who suffers from Down's Syndrome, motioned to himself that he has been struck in the head by another person.

"Who did that do you?" his mother asked. "That lady," he replied.

Ramadan was furious. For years she has been complaining to the Alexandria school system that the bus monitor on the public special needs school bus has been abusing her child. In the past she had found bruise marks on the inside of his thigh, marks that his doctor says showed that someone had pinched him severely.

This time she didn't take her complaint back to the school system. Instead, she called the police. They investigated and immediately recovered the bus video that had recorded a week's worth of travels on Ali's bus. There it was: Shawnee Keels, the bus monitor, hitting, kicking and intimidating Ali. In one rather startling scene, the bus driver and the monitor force Ali to walk to the front of the bus while the bus is in motion. He wobbles down the aisle only to be struck by Keels when he gets to the front.

Keels eventually pleaded guilty for her crimes. Ali's parents sued the Alexandria School Board for the assaults.

PATRICIA COLBY V. THE CITY OF VIRGINIA BEACH (VA)

On January 6, 1987, Patricia E. Colby was driving her vehicle east on Pembroke Avenue in the city of Virginia Beach, Virginia. As she approached the intersection of Independence Boulevard, the light controlling her lane turned green. She slowed, looked to the left and right, and, seeing and hearing nothing, proceeded into the intersection. In the middle of the intersection, her car was struck on the left side by a Virginia Beach Police Department vehicle operated by Officer William H. Boyden. As a result of the collision, Colby received serious and permanent injuries.

Shortly before the accident, Officer Boyden observed a vehicle traveling south on Independence Boulevard run a red light at the intersection of Independence and Witchduck Road. He began to pursue the offender and activated his emergency lights. He saw the vehicle move from lane to lane at a high rate of speed and subsequently run the red light at the intersection of Independence and Pembroke. Continuing his pursuit, Officer Boyden activated his siren for a short burst as he neared the intersection of Pembroke and Independence. Although the traffic light was red, he proceeded to cross the intersection. As he entered the intersection he observed Colby's car also entering the intersection. Officer Boyden applied his brakes and swerved in an unsuccessful attempt to avoid the collision.

Patricia Colby sued Officer Boyden and the City of Virginia Beach for her injuries, alleging that he was negligent in engaging in a "hot pursuit" under the circumstances.

ROBBY NIESE V. THE CITY OF ALEXANDRIA (VA)

In the summer of 1998, Robby Niese was allegedly raped on multiple occasions by an on-duty Alexandria, Virginia, police officer who was attempting to help her with behavioral difficulties that her son, Steven, was experiencing.

She reported the first rape to a counselor employed at the city's Department of Mental Health, to another city department, and to the Alexandria Women's Health Clinic. Despite her numerous reports to various city agencies, she was raped by the perpetrator on two subsequent occasions. The officer was later terminated from his job.

Niese sued the City of Alexandria. She alleged that the city was responsible to her because the officer raped her while on duty and because the city failed to act on her complaints to prevent the subsequent rapes.

CHARLEY JONES V. LOCAL VIRGINIA COUNTY SCHOOL SYSTEM[1]

Sixteen-year-old Charley Jones suffers from a rare form of muscular dystrophy and is confined to a wheelchair. Each morning a county school bus for special needs students arrives at his house to take him to school, where he takes all "honors" courses and is the manager of three of the sports teams. On May 11, 2010, the special attendant whose only job is to make sure Charley is safe on the trip to school fails to properly secure the belt that keeps his wheelchair stable.

When the bus stops suddenly, he is thrown from his wheelchair. Unable to protect himself, he falls, fracturing his leg. He develops a blood clot that travels to his lungs, almost killing him. After weeks in the intensive care unit in Children's Hospital in Washington, DC, he survives, but his parents have incurred more than $130,000 in medical bills.

His parents claim the bus attendant and the county are responsible for his life-threatening injuries.

WHAT DO ALL THESE LAWSUITS HAVE IN COMMON?

In each of the above cases, the courts held or will hold that the defendants *could not be held responsible* because they were immune from suit, either because they were charitable organizations (Didlake and YMCA) or because they were governmental "sovereign" organizations (the cities and the school board.) Thus, in each case, the injured person was left to fend for themselves because the wrongdoers were immune

---

1 The names of this case are the only ones that are fictitious, as the matter is still pending. The other cases are all publically reported cases.

from suit under the "laws" of *charitable immunity* and *sovereign immunity*.

Lawyers took on these cases knowing that their chances of prevailing were slim because, while in the past there may be been a reason to protect charities and the "sovereign" government, those days have long passed, and these lawyers are doing what they can to change the system for the protection of all. Today, these laws persist, even though most Americans believe that the consequences of carelessness should be born by the guilty and not the innocent.

Charitable Immunity
Made up by judges, charitable immunity is taken from ancient English common law. It applies to some but not all charities. It only works "against" someone who has "benefitted" from the charity. Thus, when a carelessly driven van operated by a driver employed by a business like Didlake hits and injures another person, *that* person can sue and recover damages from Didlake and its insurance company, but should one of Didlake's mentally disabled "clients" in that van suffer further catastrophic injury, he and his family are on their own paying for his injuries, even though companies like Didlake all carry liability insurance.

The usual arguments for charitable immunity are along the lines that "paying damages would violate a donor's intent or dissipate funds that might otherwise be used for the needy. Of course, all those "reasons" fail when you consider that the only victims who cannot recover from a charity's careless act are the very people the charity purportedly exists to help? Only those injured drivers in the car hit by the charity's van are able to collect their damages. Thus, ironically, the employees of the charities have *less* incentive to act carefully toward their "customers" than any other business.

Courts have been amazingly reticent to change charitable immunity laws because they say the law has now become a part of public policy.

Sovereign Immunity
Sovereign immunity means "you can't sue the government" and, in most cases, you can't even sue employees of state and local governments, either. The doctrine, like the one protecting charities from suit, is rooted in the centuries old common law of England. It was originally based on the belief that the King can do no wrong. In modern times,

it's more often explained as a rule of "social policy," which protects the state from "burdensome interference with the performance of its governmental functions" and preserves its control over state funds, property and instrumentalities. The threat of litigation, its proponents contend, may hamper or prevent a government's ability to act.

This is nonsense in this day and age.

Like charitable immunity, the doctrine of sovereign immunity places the burden of loss directly on innocent victims of the negligence of government employees.

While it might make sense to say you can't sue the sovereign for its policies, it makes no sense to protect the bus monitors on public school busses or police officers who negligently cause harm carrying out their duties.

WHAT CAN YOU DO?

Obviously, times have changed. What might at one time have been good for King Louis IV isn't good for Americans. Besides, since when is "that's the way we've always done it" a good reason for still doing something?

The general rule in the law is that if your own carelessness causes harm, then you're responsible to the victim for the harm you caused. When individuals (and governments and charities) are held accountable for their wrongdoing, they *begin to think about how they could do things better and more safely for those over whom they have responsibility.* That way, innocent victims of corporate and governmental carelessness don't have to bear the full burden of their medical bills, which today can mean financial ruin, the loss of a house and bankruptcy.

The tragedy of the "immunity laws" is that no one knows about them until a loved one is killed or injured. Most people are astonished to know who the law really protects when they bring their cases to us.

You need to voice your concern. *You* need to write legislators. *You* need to protest in your local media when you hear of these situations. Heck, send them a copy of this book and put a stickie on this chapter! You need to do this before the sweep of immunity send you or someone you know into bankruptcy!

About Ben

Ben Glass, Esq., is a best-selling author, personal injury and medical malpractice attorney in Fairfax, Virginia, who has been seen on NBC, CBS, ABC and FOX affiliates around the country as well as in the *Wall Street Journal, USA Today, Newsweek,* and many more as one of America's PremierExperts. Besides running his own firm, he is the founder of Great Legal Marketing, a firm that teaches "effective, ethical and outside the box" marketing to lawyers in small firms across the United States. He can be found at: BenGlassLaw.com and at: GreatLegalMarketing.com. You can also follow him on Facebook at Facebook.com/LiveLifeVeryBig.

CHAPTER 24

Nursing Home Neglect: How to Spot It and Stop It

Provided For Gacovino & Lake*

Moving a loved one into a nursing home can be incredibly stressful. There are so many things to worry about, from possibly convincing a reluctant parent to give up their home to dealing with the logistical issues involved. However, the biggest stressor of all may be wondering if your loved one will be properly cared for.

When you move a parent or other relative into a nursing home, you trust that facility and its staff to meet all your loved one's needs—for nourishment, comfort, and medical care, and for the bulk of their companionship and emotional support. So it can be especially troubling to hear about the adverse conditions and abuses present in some nursing homes. Fortunately, there *are* steps you can take to make sure you select the right facility in the first place, as well as how to deal with any issues should they come up.

As personal injury lawyers, we've seen too many seniors suffer at the hands of their caregivers. That's why our firm is dedicated to helping victims and their families. In the following chapter, we'll explain how to choose the right nursing home, warning signs to look for, and finally, what you can do if you're seeing something that's very wrong.

This chapter was researched and assisted on behalf of Gacovino & Lake by Celebrity Branding Agency. The attorneys at Gacovino & Lake are admitted in New York, New Jersey and Connecticut. The information provided may not be applicable in your state.

AN OUNCE OF PREVENTION

The best way for you to protect your loved one from nursing home abuse and/or neglect is to do your homework before you choose the home where he or she will be living. That means spending a considerable amount of time and energy researching any nursing home you're considering in advance—taking initiative and actually "investigating" the home beyond the typical guided tour where an employee shows off the home's best points.

To be sure you get a clear and comprehensive view of a nursing home's suitability to take care of your loved one, take the following steps:

Step 1: Tour the Facility

Nursing homes are usually at their best at those times when they're most likely to schedule an "official" visit—during a weekday. There are usually more people working during weekday shifts, meaning more people are available to keep the facilities clean and attend to residents' needs. It makes sense then that you'll learn a lot more about a facility if you visit on a weekend, when staffs tend to be smaller—or even at night, when more problems tend to occur.

It's also helpful to schedule a visit during mealtime and observe residents who are being fed. You can even ask to eat a meal yourself to judge the food's quality. Drop by the dining room and see how many residents appear to be especially thin; if there seem to be more than a few thin residents, take that as a warning sign. Check on the residents who are fed in their beds. How much time do the aides spend with each resident, and how much of the food is eaten? Are the trays sitting in front of the residents without anyone assisting them? Are the aides running from room to room trying to feed bedridden residents? Is the food cold?

Step 2: Meet the Staff

When you schedule a visit to a nursing home, you'll most likely be met by a marketing director who will take you on a guided tour and offer prepared remarks about the home's facilities, amenities and activities. This is fine for an overview, but to get a real idea of how a home functions, schedule a meeting with the home's administrator. See if you can also meet with the medical director; if you can't, find out how often he or she sees the residents—daily, weekly or monthly. Sit down with the director of nursing and ask how many registered nurses and aides work during each shift, especially at night when most problems occur.

Other important questions to ask include:

- How many staffers work each shift: morning, evening, nights and weekends? What's the staff-to-resident ratio?
- How many nurses and how many certified nursing assistants (CNAs) are on duty?
- How many residents live in the home?

Step 3: Meet Residents and Their Families
To get a clear picture of the pros and cons of a particular nursing home, it helps to talk with people who are *not* on the payroll. Obviously, if you have friends or family members who have relatives living in a nursing home, you'll want to find out whether or not they recommend it and why. If they've experienced difficulties, you may very well have similar problems.

Even if you don't know anyone with a relative in a nursing home, you can certainly ask to meet and talk with a current resident to discuss their experiences living in the home—specifically, what they think of the responsiveness of the staff, the quality of the food, and any issues they might have. You can get an even more complete picture if you talk with a resident's family and ask about their experiences.

You can also walk up and down the halls and talk to residents who aren't pre-selected by the staff, especially people who are bedridden or wheelchair bound. When you talk to residents, observe their grooming, skin quality, nail care and oral care. See if they appear upbeat or if they're depressed. If almost everyone you talk to is confused and unable to have a normal conversation, this could be cause for concern. If a nursing home restricts your access or limits you to residents of their choosing, that's another warning sign.

Step 4: Check the Official Record
By law, all nursing home facilities are inspected annually. Contact the Centers for Medicare & Medicaid Services to learn how any home you're considering has fared during those inspections. You can access these reports at www.medicare.gov/nursing/Overview.asp. If you prefer, you can call (607) 367-2101. Medicare regulations also require that

each facility have the latest state survey of the facility readily available for review.

WARNING SIGNS

Unfortunately, even the most diligent person can't always spot a problem nursing home facility. As shocking and unpleasant as it sounds, the reality is that some nursing home patients have been known to experience a wide variety of problems, ranging from neglect to emotional and even physical abuse. And since so many nursing home residents have limited abilities to communicate, this type of abuse can often go on unnoticed and/or unreported.

So how do you know if your loved one is being victimized? First, make sure you visit frequently and at different times, and when you do, keep your eyes and ears open, ask questions, and encourage your relative to be open and honest.

If this isn't possible, or if you're still unsure, look for signs. Some of the more commonly observed signs of physical abuse include:

- Unexplained injuries
- A condition the caretaker can't adequately explain
- Open wounds, cuts, bruises or welts
- Resident reports being slapped or mistreated

Possible signs of verbal or emotional abuse may include:

- Appearing emotionally upset or agitated
- Withdrawing and refusing to communicate
- Unusual behavior (sucking, biting, rocking)
- Humiliating, insulting, frightening, threatening behavior toward family and friends, or ignoring them altogether
- Wanting to be isolated from other people

Other signs to look for if you think nursing home abuse or negligence has occurred include the following:

- Injuries requiring emergency treatment or hospitalization
- Any incident involving broken bones, especially a fractured hip

- Any injury occurring during or shortly after an episode of wandering (including outside the facility) when the staff isn't aware that the resident is missing for some period of time

- Heavy medication or sedation

- Rapid weight loss or weight gain without physician or family notification and a change in treatment being provided

- An incident where one nursing home resident injures another resident

- Resident is frequently ill, and the illnesses aren't promptly reported to the physician and family

KNOW YOUR (LOVED ONE'S) RIGHTS

All nursing home residents have rights protected by the Nursing Home Reform Act and the Americans With Disabilities Act, including:

- **The right to access information, including:**
  - information on all services available and the charges for those services
  - information on the facility's policies, procedures, rules and regulations
  - information about how to contact their state ombudsman and licensure office and advocacy groups
  - access to state survey reports on the facility
  - daily communication in their own language and assistance if there is sensory impairment

- **The right to participate in their own care, including:**
  - receiving adequate or appropriate care
  - being informed of their medical condition and allowed to participate in treatment planning
  - refusing medication and treatment and be offered treatment alternatives
  - participating in discharge planning
  - reviewing their medical records

- **The right to make independent choices, including:**
  - choosing their physician
  - participating in activities in the facility and community
  - participating in a resident's council
- **The right to privacy and confidentiality, including:**
  - private and unrestricted communication, including privacy for phone calls, mail, and meetings with family, friends and residents
  - access to any entity or individual that provides health, social, legal, and other services
  - confidentiality regarding medical, personal and financial affairs
- **The right to dignity, respect and freedom, including:**
  - freedom from mental and physical abuse
  - freedom from physical and chemical restraints unless medically necessary
  - self-determination
  - treatment with consideration, dignity and respect
- **The right to security for their possessions, including:**
  - management of their personal financial affairs
  - the ability to file a complaint with the state survey and agency for abuse, neglect or misappropriation of property
- **The right to control transfers and discharges, including:**
  - being transferred or discharged only for medical reasons, if health or safety is endangered, for nonpayment of services, or if the facility closes
  - being notified of transfer 30 days in advance (in most instances)
  - knowing the reason for transfer, the date it's effective, the location to which he or she will be discharged, and a statement of the right to appeal
  - receiving adequate preparation from the facility to ensure a

safe and orderly transfer

- having policies and practices upheld by the facility that are the same for all individuals regardless of payment source

- **The right to have concerns and complaints heard, including:**
  - presenting grievances to the staff or others without fear of reprisal
  - having grievances promptly resolved by the facility

IF YOU SUSPECT A PROBLEM . . .

If you're worried something isn't right with your loved one, there are steps you can immediately take. Start by talking to people who work at the home, including nurses and aides, about your concerns. Others you should connect with are the director of nurses, the social worker, the facility administrator and, of course, your loved one's doctor. You can also call the ombudsman, a person whose sole responsibility is to offer impartial help.

You might also want to contact your state survey agency—the division of the department of health that deals with oversight of nursing homes and enforcement of nursing home regulations in your state. You can find out who the state licensing agency is from your nursing home. They're required to provide this information to you when you place a resident in the nursing home.

If you believe your loved one is a victim of any form of abuse or neglect, you can and should file a complaint with your state licensing and certification division; they're required to investigate your complaint. If they substantiate your complaint, the agency has the authority to issue a citation against the facility, impose a fine and require corrective action.

Many family members are concerned that if they make a complaint and their relative is still in the nursing home, the facility may retaliate against the relative. These concerns should be expressed to the licensing agency who will describe their procedures to protect, to the extent possible, your family member. Move your family member to another facility, if necessary, to safeguard his or her welfare.

THE COMPLAINT PROCESS

You, or any other person, may make a complaint against any nursing home to the licensing and certification branch of the state health department and request that the nursing home be inspected to substantiate the complaint. The complaint may be made orally or in writing.

Once a complaint is received, the state agency assigns an inspector to make a preliminary review of the complaint. You'll normally be notified of the name of the inspector and proposed course of action. An onsite visit to the nursing home to investigate the complaint can take place as early as 10 working days from receipt of the complaint. By law, there should be *no* advance notification made to the nursing home under investigation. When investigating the complaint, the inspector will collect and evaluate all available evidence based on the observed conditions, statements of witnesses and a review of facility records. As a result of the investigation, the inspector will determine whether the complaint is substantiated or unsubstantiated. If the complaint is substantiated, a citation may be issued against the nursing home. Whatever the decision is, you'll be notified in writing. If you're not happy with the determination, you still have recourse. You may request an informal hearing, which will be held with the state agency and may include a representative of the nursing home. If you're still not satisfied with the results of that hearing, you may then appeal it to a higher level for review. This review process is usually done by an appeals unit, and you'll be notified of the results in writing.

If you or your loved one is a victim of nursing home abuse or neglect, you can take private legal action against the nursing home in court through civil litigation. Should you need a qualified personal injury lawyer, contact Gacovino, Lake & Associates at (888) 444-4444, 24 hours a day, seven days a week, or through our website, at gacovinolake.com to discuss the case and your options. Be aware that there are different limitations in each state on the timeframe within which legal action must be taken; a lawyer can tell you what that timeframe is.

You don't have to stand by helplessly if you suspect someone is the victim of nursing home neglect. If you do suspect neglect is happening, take the appropriate actions as soon as possible to safeguard the health of your loved ones.

About Steve

Gacovino, Lake & Associates was formed by Steven Gacovino and Edward Lake in 1993 shortly after graduating Touro Law School together. Our offices are located at 270 West Main Street, Sayville, New York. We can be reached at (631) 543-5400, or contacted through our website at www.gacovinolake.com.

The firm's primary areas of practice are plaintiff personal injury, including automobile, construction, nursing home negligence, slip and fall, wrongful death, products liability, premises liability, and pharmaceutical litigation.

The firm is associated with many attorneys throughout the country, working on some of the most complex mass tort cases in the country.

The firm's primary goal is to provide high quality, zealous legal representation to all of our clients, coupled with responsive and compassionate client relations.

Both Steven Gacovino and Edward Lake have been long-time members of the New York State Bar Association, sustaining members of the American Association of Justice, members of the New York State Trial Lawyers Association, as well as, the Suffolk County Bar Association.

CHAPTER 25

Tax Problems?
Hire an Attorney—
and Change Your Life

By Rod Polston

On a hot summer day a frail woman in her 30s and her five young boys entered our law office and waited patiently in the reception area to meet with an attorney. The woman was a stay-at-home mom, home-schooling each of her children, and was heavily involved in ministry with her church. As she sat slumped down in her chair, her years of selfless dedication to others was evidenced by her well-worn hands, her patient spirit, and her gentle eyes that had been a welcoming light to so many individuals who had crossed her path. However, on this day, she also allowed a sentiment to escape that she rarely allowed herself to feel, or more important, allowed others to see—her deep-rooted feeling of hopelessness.

Most nights she would lie in bed and her dejected thoughts would fall heavily on her mind as sleep evaded her and she tossed and turned in bed. She would try to pinpoint what had brought her to this state, as if that answer would provide a key to unlock the hold her problems now had on her life. She remembered being fiercely in love with her high school sweetheart whom she married after they graduated high school. Her husband immediately began a successful business, and they quickly started their family together. The woman was eager to be a doting and dedicated housewife and was excited to be home to nurture their children as they grew. She felt blessed by God with the life He had given her and felt it was her calling and duty to bless the lives of others. She immersed herself in her church and brought her children in tow wherever she went. She tirelessly worked for the church and generously gave of herself, her time and her resources. Her slim figure wasn't a result of time in the gym but rather from chasing after her boys, completing ministerial tasks for the church late into the night, and running the household smoothly so her husband could come home and relax.

As she sat in the reception area, her distress carried over to her boys who saw the frown on their mommy's face, her downcast eyes and her slumped shoulders. As she waited, she wondered for the millionth time if she would ever determine when her husband began his adulterous affair, if she would ever find out when his business started failing, or what moment made him decide he wanted a divorce. Until this day, she had never yet cried in front of her boys, but now she no longer had the strength to cover her misery. The receptionist indicated to her that the attorney was now ready to meet with her. She slowly rose from her chair and entered the conference room with tears streaming down her face as she faced the facts that brought her here to our office.

Her mounting problems were greater than the affair, the lack of income or divorce. The IRS was after her, too. Her husband's business had failed and owed several hundred thousand dollars to the IRS. She had received letters from the IRS and came to learn that she was also personally liable for more than $90,000 in business taxes.

Her ex-husband never told her about the tax liability or that his business was in the red. Instead, he moved in with his girlfriend and left her with their five boys to fend for themselves. With the pending divorce and no income, she'd been saving every penny she possibly could with no prospects for employment, child support or alimony in sight. Today, she'd gone to the grocery store with her boys, and after her card was declined for the meager items she was purchasing, she contacted her bank and devastatingly learned that the IRS had completely wiped out all the money in her bank account. So now here she sat, in the Law Office of Roderick H. Polston, PC, to see if there was anything he could do to help.

If you were to ask her to pinpoint the moment her life dramatically changed for the better she would highlight the moment she met Rod Polston. Immediately after she retained his services, his amazing team of attorneys, accountants, IRS enrolled agents, and case managers assured her that they would fight for her, protect her rights, and set up an agreement with the IRS that would resolve her tax problems. They told her she would no longer need to have a sleepless night over this tax liability, and she trusted them. She never had another bank levy or any further contact by the IRS. Instead the IRS contacted her representation directly, and the team of attorneys and enrolled agents devised a specific strategy for her case to ensure the optimal resolution was reached.

After several months of negotiating and appeals, an offer in compromise was approved by the IRS for which she only needed to pay $756, and the remaining balance of over $90,000 was forgiven.

Here is the client's actual letter to our office following this acceptance:

"My life changed when I came to your office! I wanted to personally express my deepest THANKS for all you have done for me and my family. When I first came to you, much of this was a surprise to me, however, you were always willing to help and explain all that was being done and the steps we needed to take to progress in my case. You never stopped helping me, you always were eager to help and even explain what I didn't understand if necessary. I believe you went above and beyond, and I felt you were genuinely concerned about the welfare of me and my boys. Please know words cannot express how grateful I am for releasing me—playing a major role in releasing me from the liability that had been attached to me! Thank You Again! I am beyond blessed by you!"

Everyone with a tax liability should be able to pinpoint retaining tax representation as the moment that changed their life for the better!

This is just one story; however, this isn't an isolated event. Rather, an entire book could be filled by the stories of each and every individual case that has retained excellent tax representation and the wonderful outcomes reached in every case.

Tax attorneys recognize that each case is unique, and we take the time necessary to devise a specific strategy for your individual circumstances to ensure the optimal resolution. We recognize that owing money is a burden on your mind, and even more so when the collector is none other than the U.S. government. Everyone has heard horror stories of how the IRS will seize your home and assets to collect on a tax liability due. Thus many taxpayers are left feeling hopeless and helpless when they find themselves owing a tax liability to the IRS that they don't have the ability to pay.

That's where excellent tax representation will assist you in navigating complex tax laws and provide you with a realistic solution to the overwhelming and fear-inducing burden of owing thousands to the IRS. Many tax law offices have a staff of attorneys, accountants, enrolled agents, and case managers who work together as a team to put together a unique strategy for your individual case.

- Are you making less money now then you were before? No problem!

- Is your liability from when you were single but now you're married and you don't want your spouse to be liable? No problem!

- Is your liability from a previous business you owned? No problem!

There are a lot of reasons for why individuals find themselves owing a tax liability, however, the most important question an office should solve for you is: *What problem is this creating in your life?*

- Do you want to pay for your daughter's wedding? There's a resolution available!

- Do you want to sell your house, but it has an IRS lien on it? There's a resolution available!

- Do you want to close your business, but you owe thousands to the IRS for business tax liabilities? There's a resolution available!

No matter what the problem, an experienced tax attorney can devise a specific strategy for your case that allows you to meet your goals and lift the fear and burden of the IRS trying to hunt you down.

Now, let's think about the situation you're in: Your tax return was filed, and you owe taxes that you don't have the funds to pay. At first it was an innocent, inadvertent failure to reserve funds for your taxes. Then penalties and interest began to accrue at an astronomical rate. You tried to save money for months, but the amount you owed grew faster than you could save. Now your next tax return has been filed and even more is due. *Now what?*

For others, it has been years since you have filed a tax return and you thought you were flying under the IRS' radar, but the IRS has begun to levy your bank accounts and garnish your wages. Now the IRS is threatening to seize your assets, and you're about to lose everything. *Now what?*

Then there are those who run a business. Business owners often fall into one of the easiest pitfalls of paying their overhead and failing to pay their taxes. It happens easily because you need to pay your employees, keep the lights on and pay your rent, and it's easy to feel as if you'll be able to catch up later on your taxes. But then you find you have one quarter with taxes due, then another, then another, then another before you realize you're going to have to take a loan out just to pay back your taxes! *Now what?*

These short descriptions don't describe every single situation we've seen throughout our years of experience, but they demonstrate that no matter what has happened, we understand. The most important thing to focus on is not the problem but rather *the solution!* There's a solution that calculates your financial constraints, allows you to keep your house, releases wage garnishments, prevents bank levies, and puts a resolution in place that takes into account your realistic monthly expenses: mortgage payment/rent, utilities, car payment, gas, tags, title, insurance, health insurance, life insurance, out-of-pocket health care costs, any court ordered payments, secured debts, student loans, child support, alimony, expenses for food, clothing, housekeeping supplies, child/dependent care costs, and your ongoing tax expense.

While the government seems to be focused on you paying the full balance due upfront, a tax attorney focuses on applying tax law to work for you and will negotiate a *realistic* resolution with the IRS that takes into account your monthly financial constraints.

Now let's look at the situation from the government's perspective: An IRS agent's job is to collect as much money as possible for the government, using whatever means necessary to get it, even if that means liquidating your 401(k) and retirement, levying your Social Security and pension income, seizing your assets, and emptying your bank account while you sleep!

In contrast, we focus on you as an individual and your life expenses. We use installment agreements, offers in compromise, graduated payments plans, currently not collectible status, and streamlined installment agreements to set up resolutions you can afford.

There's no reason any taxpayer should be at the mercy of the IRS. Your rights can be protected by hiring excellent representation. If you have a tax liability, the best decision you can make is to ensure you have tax attorneys in your corner fighting to protect you and your family. Meeting with a tax attorney can provide you with perspective on how to get out of the dangerous cross-hairs of the IRS.

However, whether you seek representation or not, here are a few key tips every taxpayer should know to strategically prepare for the best resolution possible with the IRS:

- *Stay compliant going forward!* Even if you haven't filed your tax return for *years*, start filing, beginning this year/quarter. This will show initiative on your part.

- *Get your account into compliance by filing the tax returns for the years that you haven't filed.* If you haven't filed your return, the IRS will likely prepare a tax return for you without any deductions and calculate a high tax liability. Most of the time it's in your best interest to file an original tax return on your behalf. You can call the IRS and request your "Wage and Income Transripts" to be mailed to your house. This will provide you with a list of all your earnings for each year to help you prepare your return.

- *Be sure to report all income sources on your tax returns, including gambling winnings, royalty checks, rental income, etc.* Taxpayers receive large penalties and interest for underreported income.

- *Start making estimated tax payments throughout the year.* Every three months (every quarter) make a payment to the IRS for the taxes you owe on the income you've earned in the past three months. This will show the IRS you're taking proactive measures to stay compliant.

- *Make a budget for your monthly living expenses and try to stay within your means.* The IRS website lists their standard allowances for living expenses. Review this list and see where you may be spending more than the IRS will allow. This will make it easier for you to setup an installment agreement that you can afford *and* the IRS will agree to.

- *Consider a lump-sum payment.* If you can make a lump-sum payment to the IRS to bring your tax liability below $25,000, you can setup a Streamlined Installment Agreement with the IRS without providing your personal financial information to the IRS.

- *Send a check for the amount owed if you can't file your returns on time.* If you don't file your tax return by the deadline in April, estimate how much you may owe for the year and send a check to the IRS for this amount by April.

Finally, if you have a revenue officer on your case or want to set up a more complex resolution with the IRS, such as an offer in compromise, Financial Hardship Status, or a Partial Pay Installment Agreement, hire a tax attorney who will aggressively negotiate with the IRS on your behalf, protect your rights, and ensure you're not taken advantage of!

About Rod

Rod Polston is unlike any attorney you've ever met. He doesn't bill by the hour, watch the clock, send invoices for every hearing he holds, meeting he has, phone call he makes, and research he does on your case. Rather, Rod genuinely cares about each and every one of his clients and has distinguished himself from other law firms as a place that genuinely seeks to resolve the real problem that an IRS tax liability is creating in your life.

When a client meets with Rod, he doesn't push them in and out the door like a drive-thru service, but instead he feels it's important to take the time to find out the heart of the problem created by the tax liability. Clients come to the office and say they can't sleep at night, they can't plan for the future, they want to sell their house, but they can't think about any of these things because the IRS tax liability and tax liens hanging over their head. Rod Polston, the attorneys, and enrolled agents in his office meet with clients and strategize on how they can help them meet their goals and live the life they want, free of the burden of a tax liability.

Rod has also revolutionized his legal practice by trying his best to provide clients with an up-front estimate of how much their total case will cost from start to finish, regardless of the many complications that will arise through the course of completing their case. Thousands of clients have provided his office with raving reviews to share with other prospective clients so others may also know what a wonderful experience they can expect if they chose to retain Rod's services.

Rod's personal touch and his incredible staff have enabled the office to become Oklahoma's premier tax law firm and the only place to go when you need someone to fight for your rights and negotiate a resolution with the IRS.

After working for many years as an accountant, Rod's decision to become an attorney stems from his passion to help people. Rod is extremely generous with the multiple charities, missionaries, and Christian organizations he supports year-round, and this nature is reflected in his practice.

He and his staff demonstrate an unmatched fervour and tenacity for fighting for their clients' cases. Rod not only loves the challenge of solving problems for his clients but more important finds great satisfaction in providing reassurance and realistic resolutions for taxpayers who think their options are grim.

Rod has more than 17 years of tax experience and 10 years of legal experience representing clients before the IRS and has distinguished himself as a leader and strong negotiator among both the legal community as well as among the IRS agents his office routinely works with. Rod has put together an elite team comprised of attorneys, accountants and several case managers who analyze and prepare a strategy on a case-by-case basis to ensure the best possible outcome for each individual case. Rod earnestly believes this is his calling in life and is a living example of the phrase, "When you love what you do, it's not work!"

CHAPTER 26

Bankruptcy and the IRS: Dealing With Tax Debt

By Lance R. Drury

In my Southeast Missouri law practice, I deal primarily with clients who have tax issues. The federal tax code, as I'm sure you know firsthand from your own tax experiences, is a pretty complex piece of work. It takes up almost 15,000 pages of 20 volumes, which weigh in at more than 35 pounds. That also makes it over 24 times longer than the King James Version of the Bible.

It's definitely quite a challenge to deal with all the intricate rules and regulations the IRS has in place, but it's a challenge I love to meet. I find it incredibly rewarding to find the best solution for a client who has no idea which way to turn when up against the government. As I was born and raised in the area, I feel a very personal commitment to the people I help. I was driven to become an attorney by my desire to serve others in need, and, in my almost 30 years of practicing law, I've been lucky enough to fulfill that goal many, many times.

Because the tax code is difficult to understand, many people have misconceptions about what their rights are when they find themselves faced with a significant tax debt. For instance, there's a common belief that a bankruptcy filing does *not* make an IRS debt go away. That's true in certain situations but not in others.

In this chapter, I'd like to discuss when a bankruptcy filing will discharge an IRS debt, and I'll share one real-life case that illustrates how an overreaching government can end up defeating themselves when it comes to a large tax debt.

BANKRUPTCY BASICS

First, let's start by reviewing the two different types of bankruptcy filings and what each one entails.

Chapter 7 bankruptcy is designed for individuals who wish to fully discharge their debts. However, there are limitations, particularly income related, on one's ability to use a Chapter 7 bankruptcy. In a Chapter 7 bankruptcy, you're allowed to retain certain exempt property. Most liens, however (such as real estate mortgages), don't go away and neither does child support, spousal support, student loans and certain other types of debt. A Chapter 7 bankruptcy will be listed on your credit report for 10 years from your date of filing.

A *Chapter 13 bankruptcy* is meant for those who are earning enough regular income to make payments on their debts. With a Chapter 13, those payments will usually end up being less and for a longer period than the person's current debt structure allows. The two major disadvantages to using a Chapter 13 bankruptcy to deal with a tax debt, rather than negotiating an installment agreement with the IRS, is that a fee must be paid to the bankruptcy trustee for his or her services and there will be an adverse effect on the taxpayer's credit rating (at least it's only for seven years, as opposed to Chapter 7's decade).

Filing a bankruptcy petition under either Chapter 7 or 13 gives rise to what's called an "automatic stay," which gives the debtor some breathing room from all creditors' collection efforts, including foreclosure actions. It's also one of the strongest restraints available to the taxpayer for halting IRS collection efforts.

To be more precise, the Bankruptcy Code precludes creditors, including the IRS, from starting or continuing judicial or administrative collection proceedings for prepetition debts, such as seizing property or serving levies. It also precludes the IRS from requesting payments for tax periods ending before the bankruptcy petition date, sending notices of intent to levy certain property, serving summons to collect liabilities, and creating a lien on prepetition periods. This ability to "stop the clock" is one of the main advantages of bankruptcy.

HOW BANKRUPTCY AFFECTS TAX DEBT

As I mentioned earlier, a person in certain circumstances can have all or part of his or her individual income tax liability discharged in bankruptcy. The general rules are:

1. *The tax years for which you owe taxes must be more than three years old.* For example, as of April 15, 2012, taxes for years 2008 and earlier would qualify for discharge. If an extension was filed for the overdue taxes, then the 2008 taxes wouldn't be dischargeable until October 15, 2012.

2. *You must have filed the tax returns for the years you want to have discharged at least two years before you file for bankruptcy.* Let's say the taxes were owed from the 2003 tax year, but the tax return wasn't filed until February 2010. That means the individual's taxes could *not* be discharged in bankruptcy unless the person waited to file until February 2012 or later.

3. *The tax years you want to discharge in bankruptcy can't have any additional tax assessments within the 240 days prior to your bankruptcy filing.* This means the IRS hasn't increased the amount of tax you owe for any year during the last eight months prior to filing for bankruptcy. This 240-day assessment requirement is generally only an issue when you've either been audited or had additional assessments made.

4. *Finally, your tax debt can't be discharged in bankruptcy if the back taxes resulted from taxpayer misconduct.*
Filing a fraudulent tax return or tax evasion are common instances of misconduct. As you can see, there are ways that bankruptcy can help discharge tax debt, as long as the above criteria are met. Millions of taxpayer and business tax debt have been eliminated through this practice. If you're currently grappling with a huge tax debt, you should review the above rules and consult with a tax lawyer to see if bankruptcy is a good option.

Now, I'd like to share one of my real-life cases, which demonstrates how this can work in actual practice.

BOOMERANG: HOW BANKRUPTCY BEAT THE IRS

This tax case I'm about to relate to you was my most difficult one ever in all my years of representing clients with IRS difficulties, and yet, because of the stubbornness of the revenue officers involved, it ended up having the best possible outcome.

I was representing an individual who had been wrestling with IRS issues for more than 14 years. Usually, there's a 10-year statute of limitations on the IRS collecting back taxes, but in this case, it didn't apply, as my client had entered into an installment agreement on his tax debt, which extended the debt into the 10-year window. Despite the installment plan, however, he wasn't able to keep up with the payments and ended up defaulting on the agreement.

What made this case so challenging was that the IRS was completely convinced that my client was lying to them and was using a business (in this case, an LLC) to hide tax liabilities that he owed to the IRS as an individual.

I spoke with the IRS officer assigned to my client's case. She proved to be difficult, so I brought her superior into the loop, something I always do if the initial officer won't bend. Generally, the superiors are there to help move along some kind of compromise on a case, but after several weeks of ongoing discussions with both of them, we finally hit an absolute dead end. They flat-out refused to work with him on a second installment agreement for his personal tax liability, since he had defaulted on the previous one. They saw it as an unnecessary risk. They were also fed up with his excuses for nonpayment. In their eyes, they tried to work with him for more than 10 years and weren't getting the promised results.

That meant we were left with their demand for one lump-sum payment to the IRS, representing my client's entire tax liability—no other settlement would do. That lump sum was $205,000—a bill that was obvious to me, if not to the IRS, that my client just wasn't going to be able to pay. Obviously, if he had been in a position to pay the entire liability, he wouldn't have hired me to help him through this mess.

The IRS increased the heat on him. They became very aggressive and began to initiate levies against his bank accounts. Because of their unwillingness to work with my client, he was rapidly running out of time.

The impact of the IRS levies, if they were implemented, would have been catastrophic on his business and personal life. I tried everything, and now I only saw one solution: Declare bankruptcy.

Or should I say, *bankruptcies,* since it would have to involve two stages to be successful and be a lot more complicated than a normal bankruptcy. First, the only way to immediately keep my client and his business afloat was to file a Chapter 7 bankruptcy. As you recall, a Chapter 7 bankruptcy would fully discharge any tax liability that was more than three years old. This meant that, after the Chapter 7 was accomplished, three-quarters of the $205,000 disappeared.

After my client did the Chapter 7 and received the discharge, *then* he filed a Chapter 13 bankruptcy. This *forced* the IRS to set up a payment plan for the last three years of tax liability that wasn't discharged by the Chapter 7. Yes, the installment plan that they refused to consider earlier was now imposed on them by bankruptcy court. They had to agree to the new plan—one that my client could comfortably afford.

So let's review the results of the bankruptcies. First, the IRS had to agree to the installment plan that they had previously vetoed, plus the government *also* lost out on the more than $155,000 in three-year-old tax liabilities he owed.

Still, the IRS didn't want to quit and really didn't want to lose all that money. After my client filed bankruptcy, the revenue officer showed up, unannounced, at his place of employment, demanding information concerning his assets. She ended up crying on the phone when I confronted her about her actions. I had to call her superior to make her cease and desist, given that everything was then in the hands of the bankruptcy trustee.

Battling the IRS can be difficult. They're a lot like a sleeping giant that, once awoken, won't stop coming after you even when they should. They'll take advantage of the fact that you don't know all your rights and legal options and will intimidate you into saying things you shouldn't and doing what they want you to do. That's why you should never deal with them by yourself on a serious matter.

Using a CPA to represent you can also be problematic. Accountants have no confidentiality requirements nor are they trained to be expert negotiators. CPAs, contrary to most people's beliefs, are generally not tax experts; they're accounting experts, licensed by whatever state they practice in to help with accounting problems. When they studied to become CPAs, they primarily learned GAAP (Generally Accepted Accounting Practices) and took a little tax coursework. They don't necessarily know all the nuances of IRS regulations.

You also want to be careful of the large tax legal firms that advertise on television. You could get lost in the shuffle there and not get the full attention your case demands. When considering who to hire as a tax attorney, I strongly advise you to "go local" and use someone in your area who has a strong reputation and a good track record.

Please feel free to contact me at www.lancedrurylaw.com for more information about tax issues.

About Lance

As a Missouri native, Lance Drury possesses that unique quality only present in those who choose to live their lives in the state of their birth—a complete and personal investment in the lives of the people of his community.

Lance was born and raised in Ste. Genevieve, Missouri, and moved back to the area 22 years ago. By creating a local presence in Ste. Genevieve, Columbia, and Southeast Missouri, Lance brings 28 years of legal experience to the area.

Lance has an undergraduate degree in political science and economics, a law degree, and an MBA from Washington University in St. Louis with an emphasis in finance.

Lance was driven to become an attorney by his desire to serve others in need, and he has discovered that he loves the challenge of finding the perfect solution for his clients' needs. This is reflected in the type of law he's now focusing on—helping his clients solve their IRS problems.

Having traveled to such far-away places as Eastern Europe, Japan and the Caribbean, Lance appreciates the ties that bring him back to Southeast Missouri. He's a member of the Ste. Genevieve Chamber of Commerce and has served on the Planning and Zoning Board for the city of Ste. Genevieve as well.

CHAPTER 27

History of Bankruptcy Law

By John Cimino

Bankruptcy law is the product of hundreds of years of evolution. Created at the time of the Ancient Romans and even dating back to Biblical times, bankruptcy has been a product of both tradition and changing social conditions. While most of American bankruptcy laws take their root from English Common Law created during the 1500s, bankruptcy law has shifted over time, most notably during times of great economic distress. The changes have generally been beneficial to debtors, who are able to start over financially after filing and carrying out bankruptcy proceedings.

The implementation of a standard, federal bankruptcy law took many years of change, economic catastrophe, and reform based on changing social acceptability of filing for bankruptcy. Most of the laws originally were focused on allowing creditors to recover assets, and debtors were treated very poorly. During our Colonial period, laws were fairly similar to those of England, and the only shift in favor of debtors was elimination of the death penalty. The next major bankruptcy reform was not until the 1898 Act. Federal uniformity was finally addressed, and the many variations under state law were either abandoned or incorporated. This law stood until, as a response to the Great Depression, it was modified by the Chandler Act in 1938, which allowed additional relief for corporations, individuals, and those in the agricultural industry. The next major reform was not until 1978, when the powers of the bankruptcy courts were expanded and discharge was easier to obtain. Again, there was a fallow period for bankruptcy reform until the financial downfall of the mid-2000s, when the Bankruptcy Abuse Prevention and Consumer Protection Act of 2005 was passed in an effort to stop fraudulent filings. Overall, the general trends in reform deal with Congress responding not only to financial crises, but also responding to the needs of debtors as their numbers increased with the legitimacy of lending credit to not only merchants but also individuals.

EARLY BEGINNINGS

Most of the bankruptcy laws in the United States were a product of English Common Law as established at the time of the original 13 colonies. The laws at that time were extremely pro-creditor and severely punished debtor.[1] For example, until the mid-19th century, a debtor was jailed until his debt was fully paid.[2] This was seen as civil treatment compared to the laws at the time of the Romans, when debtors could be forced to forfeit all property, relinquish their spouse, or, in extreme cases, were punished by death.[3] One can actually find references to bankruptcy in the Old Testament, where it is said that every seven years a debtor shall be released from all debt. This is called the year of the Lord's release and can be found in the Book of Deuteronomy, Chapter 15 verses 1 through 7.

Debtors at the time of Henry XIII and Elizabeth I were viewed as quasi-criminals, and all the available remedies were placed in the hands of the creditors, as opposed to the courts as they are today.[4] At this time, the creditor was the only party that was allowed to bring a bankruptcy action against a debtor, thus making all debtor participation in the proceedings involuntary.[5] Relief, rather than being for the debtor, was strictly in favor of the creditor being paid what was owed to them.[6] There was no discharge of debt, which is allowed today. The main purpose of bankruptcy law at the time was paying back creditors and had nothing to do

---

1 Tabb, Charles Jordan, *History of Bankruptcy Laws in the United States*,
  3 AM. Bankr. Inst. L. Rev. 5, p. 5-52 (1995), at 7.
2 *Id.*
3 *Id.*
4 *Id.*
5 *Id.*
6 *Id.* at 8.

with the debtor's financial status.[7] This was the basic characterization until the Bankruptcy Act of 1978.[8]

In early bankruptcy laws, the entire process was similar to that of the liquidation of a corporation. The debtor's assets were seized, valued, sold, and then the profits were split *pro rata* (according to share owed) among the creditors who brought the action.[9] Additionally, since there was no complete discharge of debt, a creditor was able to bring an individual suit for collection against each individual debtor who still had an outstanding debt.[10] This occurs when the sale of the assets were not enough to pay the entire amount owed, even if the debtor had no way of paying back the remainder.

The original bankruptcy laws from England also applied only to merchant debtors (i.e., those in the trade business). Non-merchants (individuals) were governed instead by insolvency laws, which would allow an individual's release from prison in specific circumstances and sometimes allowed them complete relief from their debt.[11] Credit at this time was rarely extended, and those who engaged in the practice were often characterized as fraudulent, and in some extremes, immoral.[12] This may be why relief was difficult.

The availability of discharge was first introduced in 1705, which in turn created a more "humane" environment. However, a debtor only obtained a discharge if they were extremely cooperative

during bankruptcy proceedings, with the uncooperative debtor still subject to the death penalty.[13] A discharge was also subject to creditor consent[14], meaning that all creditors had to agree to discharge the debtor. If they did not agree, no discharge was granted and the normal practice of selling assets to pay the debts was used.

These English laws were used as a guide when the American Constitution was being written, and as a result, a bankruptcy clause was included in the founding document. This allowed Congress the option of exer-

---

7 *Id.*
8 *Id.*
9 *Id.*
10 *Id.* at 9.
11 *Id.*
12 *Id.*
13 *Id.* at 10.
14 *Id.* at 11.

cising federal control over whatever laws the individual colonies had already instituted.

EARLY U.S. BANKRUPTCY LAWS

At the time the Constitution was written, many of the separate states had their own bankruptcy laws that were based on the ideas of bankruptcy for merchants and insolvency for individuals.[15] Though the bankruptcy clause was included in the Constitution with the purpose of creating the option for Congress to pass uniform federal bankruptcy law, very few steps were taken in the years immediately following ratification. The first uniform law was passed in 1800 as purely a creditor's remedy, and only merchants were eligible to file.[16] The law was a response to an economic crash in 1792.[17] Commissioners, who acted as a sort of bankruptcy judge, supervised the bankruptcy process and in order to receive a discharge, approval was needed by two thirds of the creditors seeking their debts to be repaid.[18] This law, however, was not permanent and ended shortly after its creation.

Uniform legislation came to a bit of a standstill. There was no federal law in place between the repeal of the 1800 Act and thecreation of the Act of 1841. During this time period, there were only limited state remedies available and no federal options to pursue.[19] However, one move Congress did make was to abolish imprisonment as a punishment for debtors on the federal level.[20] The 1841 Act was again a response to a financial downturn, and it allowed for voluntary and involuntary bankruptcy. It also extended the remedies to individuals and "all persons owing debts".[21] This marked the first time a debtor could file for bankruptcy and receive discharge with few strings attached, since creditors could only block a discharge with a written dissent filed by the majority of creditors based on how much debt was owed.[22] Also, the power over bankruptcy proceedings finally shifted from the creditors to the courts.[23] The law was repealed in 1843, but is often known as the first "modern"

---

15 *Id*. at 12.
16 *Id*. at 14.
17 *Id*.
18 *See id*.
19 *Id*. at 15.
20 *Id*. at 16.
21 *Id*. at 17.
22 *See id*.
23 *Id*.

bankruptcy law since it blended bankruptcy and insolvency actions.[24]

Between 1841 and 1898, there were minor changes in bankruptcy law. Around 1819-1820, there was little to no avenue for relief of debt due to the fact that the federal government was inactive, and the remedies provided by the states were often seen as unconstitutional as interpreted by the Supreme Court.[25] In 1867, as a response to the financial situation after the Civil War, there was another temporary federal bankruptcy act.[26] There was much attention to detail in this act due to pressures from businesses in the North and agriculturalists in the South.[27] The result was that neither debtors nor creditors were happy with the laws, and little to no progress was made toward a uniform law.[28] Most of the laws were focused on rehabilitating corporations and failing interstate entities, such as railroads.[29] The main push for a federal law did not come until the Bankruptcy Act of 1898.

THE BANKRUPTCY ACT OF 1898

The 1898 Act was the beginning of permanent, federal bankruptcy law. It stayed in place, with various modifications such as the Chandler Act in 1938, until the Reform Act of 1978.[30] The focus shifted from the payment of creditors to the relief of debtors. Filing for bankruptcy, for the first time, was urged as a relief measure for debtors.[31] This shift to debtor relief was a product of changing attitudes toward credit, commerce and bankruptcy as well as the monumental economic collapse of the Great Depression. Congress now not only addressed the relief of debtors but also began changing the procedure for filing, including which courts had jurisdiction, the creation of bankruptcy "referees" (the precursor to bankruptcy judges), the ability to file involuntary bankruptcy, and no requirement for the minimum amount of debts.[32] Additionally, the Supreme Court was now able to step in and prescribe rules, determine the forms that were necessary when filing, and outline orders for procedures.[33]

---

24 *Id*. at 18.
25 *Id*. at 15.
26 *Id*. at 19.
27 *Id*.
28 *Id*. at 20.
29 *See id*. 20-22.
30 *Id*. at 23.
31 *Id*.
32 *See id*. at 23-26.
33 *Id*. at 25.

Between the 1898 Act and the Chandler Act, there were a series of amendments to the bankruptcy laws but no fundamental changes.[34] Instead, these amendments focused on adding more grounds for discharge, determined which debts would be explicitly exempt from discharge, and increased the number of actions that could be based in bankruptcy.[35] Many of these amendments were in response to the conditions created by the Depression. Additionally, laws passed in 1933 allowed relief for municipal debtors (Chapter 9), agricultural landholders and railroads.[36] The largest change came with the Chandler Act in 1938.

With the Chandler Act, the laws became much more sympathetic to debtors, and creditors lost significant ground. The Chandler Act allowed private and public corporations to reorganize as opposed to asset liquidation.[37] It created a larger number of options for corporate debtors, including traditional liquidation, arrangement for repayment with creditors through Chapter 10, filing for an extension through Chapter 12, made reorganization an option, and allowed for relief of both secured and nonsecured debt.[38] The Chandler Act also permitted voluntary and involuntary bankruptcy proceedings.[39] The variety of relief provided was a central feature to this law and was a major influence when the 1978 Reform Act was passed.

The next major shift in bankruptcy law was not until the Bankruptcy Reform Act of 1978. This act was the cementation of federal bankruptcy law and dealt with the issue at a variety of levels. It was also the first act that was not a response to a major financial crisis.[40] Finally, the United States was moving toward a unified position on how to deal with the financial woes of its citizens.

BANKRUPTCY REFORM ACT OF 1978 AND BAPCPA

Eighty years after the 1898 Act, Congress pushed for a more uniform and structured bankruptcy law. State remedies alone and the federal legislation in place were no longer deemed adequate to deal with those fil-

---

34 *Id.* at 27.
35 *Id.*
36 *Id.* at 28.
37 "History of Bankruptcy Law," *Vault Guide to Legal Careers*,
    available at www.vault.com/articles/A-Brief-History-Of-Bankruptcy-Law-17926399.html.
38 *See* Hansen, Bradley. "Bankruptcy Law in the United States,"
    available at http://eh.net/encyclopedia/article/hansen.bankruptcy.law.us.
39 *Id.*
40 Tabb, *History of Bankruptcy*, at 32.

ing for bankruptcy. The reform included the enlargement of and creation of a unified jurisdictional system, and subsequent legislation in 1986 created Chapter 12 bankruptcy as an option to relieve struggling family farms by allowing those in that situation to slowly pay creditors back rather than lose all their land and assets.[41] Chapters 11 and 13 were also created in the package of the 1978 reform.[42] The reform also strengthened the jurisdiction of bankruptcy courts under the power of district courts and is often see as the legitimization of bankruptcy because more and more entities found it socially acceptable to file for bankruptcy under the reformed code.[43]

Since the 1978 reform, there has only been one major modification of the bankruptcy code. On April 20, 2005, former President George W. Bush signed the Bankruptcy Abuse Prevention and Consumer Protection Act of 2005 (BAPCPA).[44] The stated purpose of the law is to "improve bankruptcy law and practice by restoring personal responsibility and integrity in the bankruptcy system and ensure that the system is fair for both debtors and creditors."[45] The law most notably created a new system for classifying debtors (based on where the debtor's income falls in relation to the median income of those living in the state), ensuring that debtor's attorneys were filing reliable and accurate schedules (to ensure no fraudulent filings), and the classification for an "assisted person" was modified.[46] The bottom line is this law was created in an attempt to further regulate bankruptcy proceedings and is a change that slightly shifts to favored treatment of the creditor.

Included in the change was the new rule that one could only file a Chapter 7 once every eight years. Dating back to the Bible, one could file bankruptcy every seven years, regardless of income. Congress changed the Bible! Additionally, the "means test" required debtors to file the last two months of payroll stubs with the court and analyze the last six months prior to filing. Should your income exceed certain levels, you

---

41 *Id.* at 32, 39.

42 *See* "History of Bankruptcy Law,"
    available at www.vault.com/articles/ ABriefHistory-Of-Bankruptcy-Law-17926399.html.

43 *Id.*

44 Stern, Marc. "A Primer on Sweeping Bankruptcy Reform," *GP Solo Law Trends and News*, Vol. 1, No. 4 (Aug. 2005), *available at* www.americanbar.org/newsletter/ publications/law_trends_news_practice_area_e_newsletter_home/bankruptcy.html.

45 Taylor, Megan A., "Gag Me With a Rule of Ethics: BAPCPA's Gag Rule and the Debtor Attorney's Right to Free Speech," 24 Emory Bankr. Dev. J. 227 (Jan. 2008).

46 *See* Stern "A Primer on Sweeping Bankruptcy Reform,*" available at*: www.americanbar.org/newsletter/publications/law_trends_news_practice_area_e_newsletter_ home/bankruptcy.html.

must file a Chapter 13, which requires a 36-, 48-, or 60-month payment plan. This plan will likely result in repaying some if not all of your debt owed to unsecured creditors.

The good news is that a Chapter 13 includes provisions that will allow homeowners to strip off or eliminate second, third or other junior mortgages if their home's value is less than the balance due on their first mortgage. Some courts allow a strip-off in a Chapter 7 case, but it remains to be seen if all bankruptcy courts will allow this. There are other benefits to filing Chapter 13, including the ability to pay any back taxes as well as home mortgage arrears. Upon filing for bankruptcy, all lawsuits, IRS, foreclosure, repossessions, or other creditor collection efforts are automatically stayed or stopped.

The bankruptcy laws of the United States have changed significantly over time. Laws that were once strongly geared toward repaying creditors and only available to merchants were replaced with those that favor debtors and allow individuals to file their claims in court. The power was taken out of the hands of the creditors and, instead, vested in the bankruptcy judges of the federal district courts. Debtors are now allowed complete relief in the form of discharge of their debts, and corporate entities, municipalities, and farmers were specially accounted for in various chapters and code modifications. While relief for debtors is still the main purpose of bankruptcy law, recent reforms have granted a very slight edge toward creditors. Overall, the history of bankruptcy law in the United States has been shaped by economic hardship and the social policy of allowing people to have a "second chance" when it comes to putting their finances in order.

About John

John Cimino was born and raised in upstate New York to immigrant parents from Italy. He worked his way through college, at the University at Albany, New York, and law school. Mr. Cimino was an editor on the Law Review at Gonzaga Law School. He later attended the University of Denver School of Law, where he obtained his Masters of Taxation Law (LLM) in 1982. For a brief period, he worked as a tax attorney for the now reorganized firm of Touche Ross, where he defended taxpayers. Although he is licensed in New York, Washington and Colorado, he has primarily practiced law in Colorado since the early 1980s. He served as a chapter 7 trustee for the District of Colorado, U.S. Bankruptcy Court, from 1989 until 2001. As a trustee and consumer debtor's counsel, he has reviewed and administered thousands of cases. In one case, he collected close to $4 million from a business debtor who was attempting to hide assets in a family trust, a record recovery that still stands today. Mr. Cimino is an experienced and dedicated consumer trial lawyer who has spent his entire career successfully helping consumer debtors achieve a fresh start legally using the bankruptcy code. He is the creator of the Colorado Trial Calculator® (www.ColoradoTrialCalculator.com), a tool used by trial lawyers to compute trial deadlines. He also is the creator of Win a Free Bankruptcy™ where his firm donates a free chapter 7 bankruptcy each month to a needy Colorado family.

Visit www.CiminoBenham.com for more information or call (800) 626-6437.